Special Praise for *The Joey Song*

"*The Joey Song* is a deeply personal and intense account of a mother's journey as she attempts to cope with and understand the downward spiral of her son's life in the depths of his addiction. Her own recovery process is something that anyone with this kind of family crisis must read. As a clinician, I appreciated her insights; as a parent, I empathized; as a spiritual leader, I was impressed."

—John Baudhuin, MA, CAP
Director of Spiritual Services
Caron Renaissance

"Sandra Swenson has created a heartfelt and tender book, full of courage, honesty, and, above all, love for her drug-addicted son Joey. The book will move and enthrall every reader with this powerful story of a mother captured between fate and hope. For me, as an interventionist, *The Joey Song* should be recommended reading for all parents of young people with a substance use disorder who are struggling to find recovery. A compassionate gem to be treasured and reread again and again."

—Susanne Johnson
CAI, Certified Interventionist
Sober Coach and Lead Advocate for "Heroes in Recovery"

"Sandy Swenson tells the heartbreaking story of her son's journey into addiction with beautiful, descriptive language that captivated my interest throughout. Her powerful tale of parental love and hope will heal the hearts of others who so desperately want to know that they are not alone. While the search for the truth will resonate with those who love a child, her story of strength, determination, and hope for a miracle will remain unforgettable."

—**Cathy Taughinbaugh**
Parent Coach
Author of *Parents to Ph.D.s: 28 Interviews with People Who Share Heartache, Wisdom, and Healing from First-hand Experience with Substance Use Disorder*

"Throughout *The Joey Song*, Sandy captures an array of emotions that are universal to mothers. Not all have experienced the devastation of an addicted child—but I can guarantee that most moms will relate to her poignant descriptions."

—**Judy Herzanek/Changing Lives Foundation**
Coauthor, *Why Don't They Just Quit?*

"Every parent knows the pain of letting go as their children emerge from childhood and move into adulthood. But not every parent knows the pain, the anguish, the guilt of trying to 'heal' a child with addiction and when it's time to stop trying to fix it. In *The Joey Song*, Sandy Swenson gives everyone touched by a loved one's addiction a gut-wrenching glimpse at her oldest son's struggles and those of her family and the decision to let go to save their own lives. *The Joey Song* is a must-read, no matter where you are in your journey in trying to 'fix' your addicted child."

—**Patricia Rosen**
Publisher, *The Sober World Magazine*

"A powerful story of love and addiction, *The Joey Song* is a glimpse into a world too many people don't talk about. The reader is carried alongside Sandy Swenson as she comes to understand that her teenaged son is struggling with addiction, through overdoses and hospitals and rehabs, and, finally, letting go.

"Honest and heart-wrenching and unexpectedly hopeful, this is a must-read for anyone who loves an addict."

—Barbara Theodosiou
Founder, "The Addict's Mom"

"*The Joey Song* is a moving and touching story of the frustration and heartbreak caused by the disease of addiction. Sandy demonstrates with amazing warmth and wit that it is possible for the families of addicts to recover despite the inability of their loved ones to find recovery. *The Joey Song* will move you, bringing the terror, despair, and joy of recovery into your heart. It is highly recommended for all who want to understand and appreciate the impact of the family disease of addiction."

—Bruce Eanet
Caron Board of Directors

"Sandra Swenson shares her gripping account of her son's addiction and captures what it's like to live and love someone spiraling through this brain disease . . . the constant lies, broken promises, plausible solutions . . . the dreams and hopes dashed time and again . . . I could feel her pain, anger, hopelessness, helplessness, and desperate need to be in control."

—Lisa Frederiksen
Author of *If You Loved Me, You'd Stop!* and
Loved One In Treatment? Now What!

The Joey Song

The Joey Song

A Mother's Story of Her Son's Addiction

SANDRA SWENSON

CENTRAL RECOVERY PRESS

Las Vegas

Central Recovery Press (CRP) is committed to publishing exceptional materials addressing addiction treatment, recovery, and behavioral healthcare topics, including original and quality books, audio/visual communications, and web-based new media. Through a diverse selection of titles, we seek to contribute a broad range of unique resources for professionals, recovering individuals and their families, and the general public.

For more information, visit www.centralrecoverypress.com.

Publisher: Central Recovery Press
3321 N. Buffalo Drive
Las Vegas, NV 89129

19 18 17 16 15 14   1 2 3 4 5

ISBN: 978-1-937612-71-9 (paper)
978-1-937612-72-6 (e-book)

Author photo by Jonah Koch. Used with permission.

Publisher's Note: This is a memoir, a work based on fact recorded to the best of the author's memory. Central Recovery Press books represent the experiences and opinions of their authors only. Every effort has been made to ensure that events, institutions, and statistics presented in our books as facts are accurate and up-to-date.

To protect their privacy, the names of some of the people, places, and institutions in this book have been changed.

Cover design and illustrations by Deb Tremper, Six Penny Graphics
Interior design and layout by Deb Tremper, Six Penny Graphics

This book is dedicated to Joey and Rick.

My two miracles.

My *raison de vivre*.

Only by knowing where we've been and where we

are now can we move in a different direction.

"If I accept you as you are, I will make you worse;

however, if I treat you as though you are what you are

capable of becoming, I help you become that."

—*Johann Wolfgang von Goethe*

TABLE OF CONTENTS

ACKNOWLEDGMENTS

Rick, you've been a solid rock of love and encouragement. And Joe, our sons couldn't have dreamed up a better dad. What has been so hard could have been so much harder.

Thanks to Jill Swenson at Swenson Book Development for pulling the best possible book out of me, and to Karen Gulliver, editor and dear friend, who kept me and my words in line. Many thanks to all the others who supported my efforts in getting this book to print: Adrienne Mandel, Antonio Pittarelli, Bonnie Beavers, Carol Blimline, Carol Silverman, Christine Khan-King, Cindy Khan, David Swenson, Derek Leebaert, Eugenio Villa Nueva, Heather Frank, Jennie Swenson, Joann Petrone, John Baudhuin, Julia de Valencia Duran, Julie Swenson-Magney, Kimberly Baker, Kim Straehla, Kitty Lilly, Laura Fitzpatrick, Laura Straehla, Laurie Ward, Lisa Kinn, Marcy Silbert, Margaret Erickson, Melissa Ford, Pat Williams, Rebecca Daughtery, Richard Swenson III, Richard Swenson, Jr., Robin Delgado, Sara Irani, Sue Swenson-Hoyos, Susan Portmann, and all the gals from my delightfully discerning book group: Ava Kuo, Eileen Craig, Karen Gulliver, Lisa Krim, Mindy Weinstein, and Stephanie Proestal.

And many thanks to Central Recovery Press and my warm and wonderful editor, Helen O'Reilly, for the support and the faith and for giving my words a chance to be heard.

PRELUDE

Today Joey returns to the place where his life began.

On a stretcher.

Cruising down the coastal highway in a four-door sedan at fifty mph, Joey slammed into an SUV, a line of mailboxes, and a stone wall—no brake marks—before bouncing into oncoming traffic. He arrived here in an ambulance, bloodied and unresponsive, with enough alcohol in his bloodstream to kill him. *If his internal injuries don't kill him first.*

Twenty years, five months, and six days ago Joey tumbled into my world at this very hospital, Brevard County Medical Center in Melbourne, Florida. We greeted each other, this baby and me, but we already knew each other. We were already in love. He nestled in where he belonged, close to the heart he'd hugged for nine months, and into the arms whose most important purpose was now to protect, care for, and love.

I can't hold Joey in my arms this time. He's too wrecked all over. Too battered, bruised, and scraped. I'm afraid of hurting him, but my longing to touch Joey is greater than my fear. I find a small spot on his blood-crusted forehead where it seems safe to place a soft kiss, and I hold onto his cold, limp hand. He is so pale. So gray. So still. The only sound is the dirge of whirs and beeps and gurgles—the sucking and trickling of life's juices through a tangle of tubes and mechanical attachments.

And the whimpering.

I think the whimpering is me.

Joey fills the entire bed—the six-foot length of his body sags down the elevated slope, his legs all crumpled and akimbo at the bottom. His hospital gown reveals he is more bone than meat. Joey's hands and feet, like a puppy's paws, don't fit the rest of him. But Joey's not as thin as the last time I saw him, several months ago. Back when I told him it hurt more for me to hang on than to let go. Back when I told him I was done trying to help him until he was ready.

This is not what I thought "ready" would look like.

Joey does not move, not the tiniest bit, other than the mechanical expansion of his chest. He doesn't know I'm here, but still, I talk. I want to reach the part of him imprisoned for so many years. Maybe I can slip past the wily warden of addiction and touch Joey while he's unconscious. I tell Joey I love him bigger than the moon, that I flew here as quickly as I could, and that his dad's plane will land soon.

"Joey, you were in a car accident. No one else was injured." And then I lie. "Things will be better now."

I cannot breathe. I pray for more time.

Sitting at his side, I pat Joey's stiff and bloodied hair. Golden locks I've washed a thousand times between bubbles and boats. I no longer see the addict my son has become—a person I no longer know at all. Instead I see my little boy, snug in his innocence, transposed over this wounded, lifeless man-face. I see the glow of his smooth cheeks peeping out from under rumpled covers as I stand over his small bed late at night. A sob escapes me as I remember the little boy with the sticky giggle who one long-ago day asked me to sing him his special song.

"Mommy, will you sing me the Joey Song?"

Hmmm . . . the Joey Song?

As Joey wriggled onto my lap, his blue eyes looking up at me, I silently willed the song to come to mind.

Oh . . . the JOY Song.

My heart warmed. For countless renditions, Joey had heard my crooning as a love song—a love song about him. And so I held my little fellow tight and sang the song that had tender, new meaning; the song that was so much more wonderful sung his way.

I've got that Joey, Joey, Joey, Joey down in my heart
Down in my heart
Down in my heart
I've got that Joey, Joey, Joey, Joey down in my heart
Down in my heart to stay.

Dusting off the old song now, I lean close to Joey's ear and sing. A damp and croaky whisper. I sing the Joey Song, hoping to reach something deep within this lost child of mine. Hoping to stir up memories of love. Real love. A love so much better than the love he has for the things that feed his addiction. I want to take Joey back to a time before all the pain. I sing softly. I don't want the addict to hear.

I ache for Joey to believe what can't be seen. *These recent years have been a test of the strength of my heart, but the strength of my love has never wavered.* Not even under pressure of the mind-bending contortions imposed by his addiction.

"Joey, can you hear me? It is love that kept me from helping you to hurt yourself any longer. It is love that kept vigil while I waited for you to hit a 'bottom' that wasn't *dead*. It is love that brought me here to you now." Joey doesn't know I am here. He doesn't move.

Never could I have imagined an illness so cruel. With its insidious ways and nasty grin, addiction not only snuffed out my child's emerging light; it broke bonds and hearts and all the rules. Addiction is the destroyer of everything.

The intensive care unit nurse asks me to leave the room. She needs to do something with the tube that sucks black stuff from somewhere deep inside Joey.

Buttoning my sweater against the surprise chill of the night air, I step outside the hospital lobby. A few steps away from the door, I sit down on a bench in the shadows. My mind rummages through Joey's life for explanations.

Why is my son, at this moment, breathing only because of some machine he's connected to? Why did he slug down so much alcohol that he may never again open his eyes?

Maybe I'm fooling myself, but I see a life full of bedtime stories and family dinners, camping and fishing trips, togetherness and great opportunities. Sure, there were bumps in the road and roads not taken, but there were no ugly ogres or catastrophic events along Joey's way. Everything was so right before it went so wrong. So full and happy and promising before the destroyer of lives slithered in. *There's no reason for this tragedy.* There's nothing for me to grab onto, dammit. There's nowhere for me to put the blame.

I do see a long string of missed clues, however. Whatever was happening—whatever was brewing, growing, looming—as Joey's parents, Joe and I didn't notice, even though it happened right before our eyes and under our noses. Sort of like not noticing a child's growth spurt until many inches later. Or like not noticing the chill of the surf on your toes after a long afternoon's tumble of waves.

The pain of Joey's addiction has taken a toll on all of us: his father Joe, his brother Rick, and me over the past several years—as a family, as a married couple, and as individuals. We are like the three blind men in the fable, trying to identify the elephant by groping our way along the trunk, the tail, the leg. Each of us feeling the truth of our own experience. We rarely agree on just how okay, honest, or high Joey is at any given time, giving rise to conflict among us. Oh, the toxic corrosion of addiction.

More often than not, Joey is that elephant, and he's in our living room. Joe keeps reality at bay with loud laughs and big dreams and by running long races. Rick, after so many years of so little brotherhood, can pretend he's an only child to escape the drama of overdoses, arrests, and chaos. And I disturb everyone's peace by talking about everything until it hurts all of us with every breath. So I don't dredge everything up anymore. At least not as much.

There is healing power in putting ink to paper. It draws so much out of my mind besides words. Sleepless nights, spent roaming a dark house, are far fewer now that my thoughts, feelings, and fears are gathered into a notebook. I've finally found a way to let go of some pain—and sometimes to fuel it. A vent for the steam of my worries. I write as a way to piece together the tragedy in my family, the arrival of the future often helping me make sense of the past. And I write to remember Joey, the Joey I knew before the addict took his place. I gently fondle old memories—the fragile snowflakes of time—and put them in the safe and everlasting place of words, not to be altered or forgotten in the ravages of this ongoing storm.

I've heard it said that if you shake any family tree, an addict will fall out, and sadly I've discovered this to be true. More families are dealing with the addiction of a loved one than I ever would have guessed. The tragedy unraveling those families is similar in its destruction—different only in the details—and too often it is kept secret.

When addiction grabs a child, it chokes a parent. I know the life-draining squeeze of its grip. I've never felt so incapable and helpless, so sad, so lonely. And so afraid. My child has been stolen from me—stolen from himself—and I mourn Joey's loss and suffering from a very lonely place. There is no broad community empathy or support for the families of addicts. There is no rallying cry of solidarity, no pretty ribbon brigade, and none of the comfort that so often gets baked into meat loaves and muffins. Instead there are closed doors and mouths and minds and hearts.

I want addiction to be understood, not misrepresented, misjudged, and mishandled. Not hushed up or hidden away. Nasty things grow most freely in dark corners; the scourge of addiction needs to be dragged out into the light.

Addiction pummeled my family. Beating it back has been one long, hard fight. These mother's hands of mine, these nubby, bloodied claws, have seen battle—the battle between Hanging On and Letting Go; the battle between Barely Hanging On and Hanging in There; the battle to Survive the Unexpected; and the battle Just to Survive. Battered and bruised I may be, but I'm stronger and wiser. I finally understand there's nothing more I can do to help my son other than support him in a quest to help himself. Still, I carry around the very maternal and human need to do something. And I need to do something with this need to do something.

So, I share my story. One mother's story of love and loss and learning. And surviving my son's addiction while coming to terms with the fact that he may not.

Written from the place where I live, the place where love and addiction meet.

This is *The Joey Song*.

PART ONE

I would get to give and take and know a love bigger than
the moon, but when the time came, I would need to
love my sons enough to let them go, without hesitation.
They would need to know I believed they could fly.

~ SANDYSWENSON.COM

Verse One

IN THE CARDS

The mystic's crinkled old hands sweep my tarot card reading off the table and onto the scraggly patch of New Delhi lawn at my feet. Bangles jangling and tongue clacking, she leans forward, staring at me, I suppose, but her eyes are just shadows behind her beaded red veil. Hindi words snake out from beneath the gossamer folds and across the little hairs on the back of my neck. I don't understand what she's hissing at me, but she's made her point: Whatever she saw in the cards isn't good.

Slightly miffed, I turn my back on the ancient party-pooper; doesn't she know the fortune-telling tents have been pitched here for pure entertainment? This, most certainly, is *not* entertaining. Wrapped and rustling in a bolt of shimmering lime-green silk, I sashay back to the gala event where dignitaries, diplomats, and expats gather. Lifting the hem of my sari, teetering a bit on bejeweled heels that sink into the spongy grass, I dismiss the ominous scattering of cards with a flick and a twirl.

The sultry night air is swirled with melodic tendrils of sitar and flute. Gently swaying to the exotic music, I lean into Joe, sipping wine and tasting curried morsels offered by turbaned waiters. The starlight, lanterns, and ethnic finery outshine for a moment the garbage-picking poverty right outside the iron gates. Sighing, I delight in the fancifulness of the evening—its costumes, carpets of marigold petals, and aromatic clouds of frangipani. A Bollywood-style finale to our happy first year in India.

Slipping away before the party is over, just before the moon glides into tomorrow, Joe and I stroll the campus of the American Embassy School, the same grounds where during the week our boys huddle with friends between classes. Joey is finishing up eleventh grade and Rick is finishing eighth. Meandering arm-in-arm between flowering trees and down paved steps, as we approach the stone perimeter the revelry fades into the night. Once outside the sandbagged, armed-guard entry, Joe and I dart between rickshaws, honking cars, and cows—New Delhi is wide-awake even at this late hour—to our house just across the street. Giggling, we toss pebbles through the massive gate at the end of our driveway, aiming for the whitewashed sentry hut where our guard snoozes.

In India, every little thing is an adventure, a *masala,* a spicy blend—and I love it. As with all our moves, Joe's job brought us here. With one pinky toe on the corporate ladder before the boys were even born, he's been moving up—and so we've all been moving in, moving out, and moving on about every two years—ever since. From Florida to Minnesota, Texas to Spain, and Kentucky to India, our family has shared experiences I couldn't have imagined back in our newlywed days of a two-room apartment, one car, and no money.

Life is good. One long, smooth wave that we've somehow hopped on and are going to ride all the way to gray hair and happily ever after.

Anything different is not in the cards.

⤬

"Sandy, wake up."

I can't see Joe's face, but I can feel his fear even from under the pile of blankets. I can hear it in his voice when he tells me that Joey is down the hall in his bedroom, right now, at two-thirty in the morning, doing sit-ups in bed in the dark. Not just *doing* sit-ups. He's in a *froth* of sit-ups. And he won't stop.

There's no more hiding from the truth. We've got a son with a problem.

It's not that Joe and I have ignored Joey's baffling bits of behavior up until now, but we have been trying to shove them into a puzzle where they didn't all fit. Over the summer and first few months of his senior year— as Joey became increasingly edgy, dramatically thinner, and weird about food—we wanted to believe he was displaying teenaged, not troubled, behavior. But we were wrong.

Joey's transformation from good-natured to short-fused can't be blamed on hormones. Not entirely, anyway. And the stench from Delhi's garbage piles crawling with hairy hogs and hungry people isn't to blame for Joey's shrinking appetite. No, my son is down the dark hallway in a frenzy of self-flagellation because of something really scary. The wasted frame, the knobby wrists, the sunken eyes; I can see the truth now. Joey needs help. Help he's not going to receive in this country where having an eating disorder seems sadly ironic.

Joe and I don't know much about eating disorders, only enough to be afraid. Through a friend in the US, we get the name of a doctor in Los Angeles. Because of the time difference, it's the middle of the night when I place the call asking for guidance. As I recount Joey's recent behaviors, Joe leans in close, talking into one ear while the doctor speaks into my other. Tentatively confirming what we already suspect, Dr. Sather says he'll do a formal evaluation of Joey in two weeks, just after Thanksgiving, when a bed opens up in the inpatient eating disorder program.

"Plan for Joey to be here for several months." Stunned, I hang up the phone.

This is real and we need to make plans.

Joey was born tenderhearted. When he's around, hugs don't go un-hugged, smiles don't go un-smiled, and upside-down bugs don't go un-uprighted. Yes, Joey is an angel. Except when he's not. Lately unpredictable and explosive, Joey is more likely to slam a clenched fist into the wall and storm from the house than he is to agree with anything or to share a smile. So, if Joey doesn't like the idea of being locked up in a faraway hospital, Joe and I agree there's no way we'll get him there. Shrinking though he may be, Joey is still a sizeable young man bursting with stress, testosterone, and whatever else is going on inside him. To get him help, we must first get him on and then off a couple of planes and halfway around the world. For us to accomplish this, Joey must be willing to travel. The thought of Joe needing to use his size and strength to contain or restrain Joey on our upcoming journey slips my soul off its axis. So, in the spirit of safe and happy travels, Joe and I agree to lie.

Herding Joey into the little sunroom where I sit picking at my cuticles, Joe nudges the door shut behind them with the toe of his shoe. Cornered upon his return home from school, Joey's face is taut, teeth clenched, but still, I'm struck by his poise and strikingly handsome good looks. How is it possible for someone so sick to look so good? And just yesterday, Joey spent an hour patiently working a ring off my too-fat finger, cringing when I cringed, and murmuring gentle words of comfort. He wasn't cranky or explosive at all. *Maybe Joe and I have figured things out all wrong.* Taking a deep breath, I give Joey a fake smile and pat the sofa cushion beside me, but, caged and wary, Joey ignores me and starts to pace. Following him with my eyes, I give him the fake truth.

"Honey, your dad and I are worried about you. You've gotten so thin. It's very possible that while living here in India you've contracted an intestinal parasite. Giardia, maybe. We've made an appointment with a doctor in California to have your weight loss evaluated. We'll both go with you, we'll figure out what's going on, and we'll have you back here in no time."

Bellowing, Joey whirls around and smashes his fist into a picture on the wall. Glass shatters. Dots of blood roll from his hand onto the floor. Shouting hateful words, he roars down the hallway and slams his bedroom door. I try not to think about what his reaction will be once he discovers the truth.

"We did the right thing. We needed to lie. We must do whatever it takes now, if there's even to be a later to deal with," I say to Joe. And myself.

⁓

"Joe, it's time!" I'd hollered, flicking dust bunnies off my small hospital bag as I waddled out the door before him.

College sweethearts, Joe and I married, mortgaged, and matured a few years before starting a family. Then, it was with goose bumps and awe that we watched the shadowy ballet of our child moving and growing inside me. We posted every ultrasound image on our refrigerator. We giggled our way through Lamaze classes, panting and practicing for the big day. And we embraced the concept of "pain with a purpose."

No drugs for our baby.

Our firstborn son, Joey. Nine pounds zero ounces of solid miracle.

When Rick was born two years later, I had a miracle for each hand.

As different as the sun and the moon, my boys shine on the world with their own special light. Joey is thoughtful and opens doors for old ladies and likes to bake cakes and plan celebrations for the people he loves. He grills up a great steak, and would rather fish than sleep. He has a chiseled face and a smile that melts hearts, and with his fair complexion and blond hair he takes after me. Rick is funny, easygoing, and loyal. He likes noise and winning at games, prefers to eat things that can be dumped out of a box, and does not like to waste time on things like cleaning house. With his thick head of dark hair and eyes the color of rich cocoa, he's a near replica of Joe.

Life before children was like singing a song without knowing the words, or like knowing soft without having touched a puppy's forehead. My days were far less full-bodied then, but I didn't realize that until I had Joey and Rick. A first-grade teacher before my children were born, I have had the full-time job of "Mom" ever since. I wanted to be home to catch a glimpse of the unexpected precious moments—and to put a halt to the not-so-precious ones, too. Because our family moved on to a new state or country with near-biannual rhythm, there seemed to be a constant need for beds, balls, bodies, and beginnings to be hustled along and settled in. My boys have brought out the best in me and the worst in me—they've brought out *all* of me—and I'm more the person I was meant to be for having been their mom.

With Joey now seventeen and Rick almost fifteen, their childhood is just the bulb from which they blossomed. But, along with their treasured Teddy and Blankie, it's tucked away in a special place for safekeeping.

I can only imagine where I'm going to want to tuck teenhood.

We cancel our Thanksgiving trip to the Camel Fair in Pushkar, making up an excuse for our staying close to home instead of saying to the boys that we fear Joey might keel over in the middle of the desert.

Just as it's not easy tricking Joey into going to an eating disorder clinic, it's not easy to trick him into completing his college applications early so he won't miss the deadlines he doesn't know he's going to miss.

"Joey, if you earn a college scholarship, and complete the requirements for Eagle Scout, we'll give you a car for graduation. And if you get your college applications done in the next two weeks—before we leave for California—we will take you to look at cars while we're there," I say.

"Just think, you would be able to use your car for getting to work or getting away from campus for some camping and fishing," adds Joe. "As long as you take a full load of classes, maintain at least a B average, and don't ever drink and drive, the car would be yours."

Joey is thrilled about the possibility of car shopping in a few weeks.

Bribery accomplished.

I've collected a suitcase full of schoolwork from Joey's teachers that will hopefully keep him on track to graduate while he's hospitalized for his eating disorder. There's been speculation on campus that the decline in Joey's appearance and mood might be due to drug abuse. *Thank goodness that's not the case.* I've heard that drugs are easy to come by here—as easy as signaling to a certain dented green rickshaw circling outside the school gate—so I guess things could be worse.

⁂

India. She's a beauty. So colorful and proud, she wears even poverty and overcrowding with a certain grace. But the need in India is overwhelming—and so, I've been trying to save babies for the past year. What started as the holding and feeding of orphans evolved into learning about afflictions such as anal fistulas, clubfeet, and hearts with holes, and then raising money to change the fate of the little orphans who have them. It evolved into the Moms' Circle of Love, a circle of loving expats all volunteering their time to the same cause. Now, before my departure, I'm handing off baby Prisha—one of the orphaned babies who brightened our home for weeks and months pre- and post-life-altering surgery—to one of the other substitute moms.

Have I been too busy with sick babies to see the sickness in my own son? So much for my oft-spoken motto, "Love Begins at Home." *What other things have my boys seen me do that were at odds with what I said?*

I would never have allowed them to eat a whole bag of Oreos in an hour or only salads for a week—but I have done both. "Love yourself for who you are," I told my sons, while not ever finding myself quite right—always either too thin (once) or too fat (more than once). *Did I flip-flop Joey into an eating disorder with my mixed messages?* I crashed the car once because of an immediate need for lipstick. *Will my boys now disregard that thing I keep telling them about keeping their eyes on the road at all times?* I tried yoga once, but when I planked it was only in my mind; I looked like a log—but I was a quitter. *Oh, what have I done that can't be undone?*

The short years of childhood don't allow much time for slapping down the solid brick-and-mortar foundation of fulfilled and capable adults. I tried. I had good intentions. But I messed up—a lot. I guess I always hoped some cosmic scale would balance out all the rights and wrongs. Or some benevolent scorekeeper would just look the other way once in a while. Now I guess I hope I'm right.

In leaving India with one son, I leave the other behind. That there's no real choice in my doing so doesn't make this any easier. Even though Rick will be in the caring hands of my friend Cindy and her family until Joe's solo return, I'm leaving him parentless in a foreign country. I feel sick not knowing when I'll see him again. Dropping him off at his temporary home, I walk Rick to the front door. He's ready to make a quick good-bye of this, but I don't care. I take a deep breath and freeze the moment. Closing my eyes, I inhale the aroma of chocolate mixed with boy sweat, and I memorize the feel of barely-there bristles rubbing against my cheek as I hold my young son close.

The trip from New Delhi to Los Angeles via Beijing lasts twenty-seven long hours. Nerves stretch over the thousands of miles like ribbons of silk caught and pulled by the wind until frayed to threads. Joe and I never discussed whether he would make this trip with me; we didn't need to. He's always been there for his sons—from changing diapers to pitching tents to just hanging out doing nothing at all—and this wouldn't be any different. Joey's not in any mood to appreciate that, but I do. Wedged between my taut-jawed travel companions, I pretend to read and eat and sleep, and I pretend we're a happy family, countering Joey's snappishness with sweetness or eye-contact-avoidant silence. My elbow brushes Joey— the tightly wound bundle of sticks sitting to my left.

"Get off me," he sneers, jerking his arm away. As though I've stabbed him. "I can't believe you're making me see this doctor. I'm not sick. You'd better make reservations as soon as we land to have me back on a plane to Delhi right after the appointment tomorrow." When we finally land, Joey is so tense that he appears even more shrunken than his already shrunken self. I'm surprised he makes it all the way to the hotel before snapping.

Jet-lagged, rumpled, and weary, I roll my suitcase across the gray-green mottled carpet and do a quick assessment of our room—two queen beds, a small sitting area, a view of the hospital beyond a little terrace filled with potted plants. Joey tosses his suitcase onto the floral bedspread nearest the door as Joe lifts his onto the folding luggage rack in the closet. I peek into the bathroom at the shower and soap.

"Who wants to go first?" I ask, turning to beam my smile upon the first chivalrous responder. But Joey is gone. I catch just a glimpse of his sneaker as he darts out the door toward the dark streets of this unfamiliar city. Joe and I don't budge, or even blink. Time is sucked out the door behind Joey. It is seconds or minutes or hours before we start to bump around, yelling at each other to do something. Joe runs after Joey. I stay behind because we can't find where we put any of the room keys. It's only a few minutes until Joe returns, out of breath and empty-handed. He saw Joey running far ahead on the sidewalk but couldn't catch up. When he called out, Joey took one glance over his shoulder and ran faster.

Joe and I shout about what we should do and which of us should do it, but our room soon turns quiet. There is nothing for us to do. Nothing but wait. And pace. And hope that Joey comes back. So that's what we do. Hours later, when there's a knock on the door, Joe and I trip over each other to open it. Joey enters, flicks away our questions, and collapses on his bed without a word. Rolling toward the wall, he pulls a pillow over his head. Turning out the lamp on the nightstand, Joe and I sit on the edge of our bed. We whisper and wait for the rough cadence of our son's deep-sleep breathing. Finally, tiptoeing, we move around the darkened room, creating a tipsy mountain of suitcases and shampoo bottles in front of our hotel room door. Now, if sleep does come, we'll be awakened if Joey attempts another escape during the four hours until sunrise.

Nobody eats the hearty breakfast served outside on the terrace under the warm December sky that nobody notices. We just move the sausages and eggs around on our plates until it's time to depart for Joey's appointment. The three of us trudge across the street to the sprawling hospital, but only two of us know what's coming. (I'm only trudging on the outside; on the inside I'm running away.) The closer we get—to the glass doors at the main entrance, to the sign aiming us to the psychiatric ward on the sixth floor, to the metal door behind which he'll be locked up—the more halting Joey's steps become. And the harder it becomes to keep my trembling knees from folding. I watch as my son's grudging trust turns to rabid anger at the realization that he's been duped. A whirling dervish of elbows and legs, Joey turns on me, face twisted and pleading. As he's taken away by the white-coated staff trying to restrain him, I claw at the air between us, crying, begging Joey to understand what is to him an inexplicable betrayal.

Weighing in at 138 pounds, down from a normal of 190, and measuring a heart rate of thirty-eight, Joey's vital signs indicate that he's a sick young man indeed. The medical team prescribes three to six months in the eating disorder program. If Joey weren't so weak, he'd blow a gasket.

Several days later, Joe returns to India and to Rick. Eventually, I move into a beigely appointed efficiency apartment within walking distance of the hospital. Visiting hours are from four to six o'clock in the evening, but that only matters if Joey deigns to see me. I fawn over him as much as I can to make up for my big fat lie and for him being so sick.

Christmas passes. The New Year begins. The days, weeks, and months crawl by. Joey gains some weight, but becomes manipulative and mean. There's an aura of smug shadiness around Joey—nothing sharply defined— but a mother knows things.

Something in Joey is slipping away.

Gasp.

The cards. Is what's happening to Joey what spooked that moth-eaten old fortune teller in India?

Bewildered, lonely, and terrified, I don't know what Joe and Rick think or feel about anything. And I don't even care.

After three long months of captivity and self-pity, it's springtime when Joey is discharged from the eating disorder program and the two of us reunite with New Delhi. We silently embrace the roadside vignettes on the ride home from the airport—bicycles stacked with entire families; red-bottomed monkeys lolling in the heat; sugarcane- and chai-wallahs hawking their wares. *Home.* But not for long. It doesn't seem like a good idea to remain in India after the end of the school year with Joey heading off to college in the fall.

Joey appears less sunken and shrunken, but he has no understanding of what happened or why. And neither do I.

"I ate what they wanted me to eat, did what they wanted me to do, and said what they wanted me to say—anything to get the hell out of there." That's what Joey told me on the plane. Whatever it takes, I guess.

All that matters is that my healthy Joey is back.

With the help of family and friends, Marines from the American embassy across the street, fellow Boy Scouts, and our Indian cook, driver, and sweeper, Joey designs and builds a wooden play fort for kids at a local orphanage—his Eagle Scout project. At his Court of Honor ceremony, surrounded by many of the same faces, Joey solemnly accepts his badge. Standing tall and proud, he is presented with an American flag flown over the very embassy in which we gather. Celebrating this moment that is, as much as having dodged this moment that almost wasn't, I fight back tears. My son has made it; he has survived the wild ride of adolescence, stronger and better for it. Today the real Joey shines—both inside and out. He gives a brief speech.

"Mom, you are the most amazing person I know. Out of everyone, we are the most alike. Because of this you always know when I need help, or just a loving hug. There have been times when I've thought I didn't need help, but it was you who showed me that I really did. The last months have been hard, but in every struggle you've been there for me, never giving up, even when I was ready to. For seventeen years you've been my best friend, and not once have you let me down. I know you'll always be there for me, and I want you to know that no matter how far apart we are, I will always be there for you. Thanks for everything you've done for me; every hug, every word of encouragement. Thank you for being my mom."

With multiple college admission offers and academic scholarships to choose from, Joey sets his sights on his high school graduation and life's next great verse.

Life is good. I feel silly for having given the old mystic and her tarot cards a second thought.

Verse Two

SILENT SCREAM

In the smallest hours of this not-yet-dreadful morning, I'm snug in my bed in Bethesda, Maryland, tangled in a tumble of pillows, Joe's arms, and dreamy dreams. Such a cozy cocoon. Until I roll over to answer the phone.

I hear the voice of an old family friend, but don't want to hear what she's saying.

"Joey's in the hospital. He was drunk and then swallowed a bottle of pills. The emergency room doctor is pumping his stomach now. Sandy, he was trying to kill himself."

My heartstrings stretch the miles to where my son lies in San Diego, California.

"Hold Joey's hand. Even if he can't hear you, please tell him I'm coming."

Clutching my head in my hands, I cry without breath, without sound. Turning my face upward, I struggle to set free the anguish that's jammed inside my chest, my throat, my being, but I've no strength to propel it forth.

A mother's silent scream.

Maybe I should have seen this coming—after all, the launch of Joey off to college was sputtering, at best.

Maybe I should have.

But I didn't.

Joe is awake now and sits up, his face twisted like the confusion of sheets and blankets around us. I want him to turn the lamp back off so I won't have to see his face when I tell him his firstborn son just tried to take his own life.

⸜⸝

As dawn takes its first groggy peek at today, I'm airborne, squashed between bulky shoulders and behinds on my way to Joey's suicide-attempted side. To the gurney where he lies retching against long, rubbery tubes—the poison from his belly more easily sucked away than the poison in his spirit that will be left behind.

Why is life so hard for my child? So damn hard?

Yesterday Joey called to tell me about his first week of college, but he didn't tell me about the desperation right underneath his cheerful veneer. *Why didn't he know I could handle—and could help him to handle—the truth? Why didn't he know I would want to know he was hurting? And why didn't I already know?*

There have been signs Joey is struggling. I've seen them. I've felt them. But I didn't know what to do with them. Between the reentry from India and the send-off to college, summer was wedged like a contented sigh—full and pleasant. Lured, lulled, and giddy, I wanted to believe Joey was one happy and productive adult-child, ready to launch.

I wanted to believe that the end of the eating disorder episode meant the end of all problems forever. But then he was arrested for driving 103 mph (with marijuana in his pocket) while driving from East Coast to West, on his way to San Diego University (SDU) in California. He took anger and manipulation to a new and hideous level when Joe and I put his car into storage. And he quit and un-quit college several times over the days we were there to help him move into the dorm. Yes, the college send-off-from-hell was full of signs. So maybe I shouldn't be stunned that my child tried to commit suicide. But I am.

Later this morning, Joe will serve up the latest bad news to Rick along with his toast. It was only last week that Rick started his sophomore year at his new high school (in a new town, state, and country) and Joe started his new job. While yesterday seemed off to a good, solid start, today begins on shaky ground. We've moved so frequently that we're adept at adapting, but that's because we lean on each other, and now I won't be there, for I don't know how long, to help smooth kinks and soothe worries.

The plane curves in for a landing, tilting its wings over the sparkling San Diego Bay, a view Joey would see from his dorm at SDU this morning if he weren't comatose in some emergency room.

Except, it turns out, he's not.

It is Joey's lanky form that unfolds from the backseat of the green SUV idling at the curb. Somehow, he's here at the airport to meet me, sprouting a single row of vacuum-cleaner-like bristles from his otherwise hairless head. I'm oddly struck by the thought that Joey's gray pallor, his stubble, and his bruised-looking eyes suit his new Mohawk quite nicely. As quickly as I grab him up into a tight squeeze, I push Joey away for inspection. A scrap of bloodied gauze is taped on his arm; there's a bit of yellow crud stuck in the corner of his mouth; his eyes have no spark.

"Thank God you're alive and standing here. But what the hell?"

I'm furious.

My son's cry for help was bounced out of the hospital in less than twelve hours.

"Where's the diagnosis? The prescription? The plan?"

"Mom, I'm fine. I was drunk. Trying to kill myself was a mistake. I'm glad you came, but I don't want to talk about this."

"Well, Joey, that's not an option."

❧

Whether it's to please me or shut me up doesn't matter—Joey agrees to be evaluated by a doctor at a nearby psychiatric hospital. With strings attached, of course.

"I will talk about what happened, but I will not go to the loony bin."

I have no way of knowing what the doctor will advise, but I look Joey straight in his trusting blue eyes, and I lie. Because, as with the eating disorder, Joey has to get through the door to get the help. Whatever kind of help that may be.

"Joey, this appointment is for you to talk through what happened. Nothing more."

Rebecca—the old family friend who's been sucked into our drama—drives us to the appointment, and as she pulls her SUV into the parking lot I can see Joey appraising the big granite block of a building that looks uninvitingly cold even in the late-summer heat. As she eases the car into a tight space, Joey flings open the back door and runs across the asphalt with the long, swift stride of a hunted deer. He's gone, up and over a grassy berm, out of sight and heading toward the freeway before the keys are out of the ignition. Gone. I start to fumble at my door handle, ready to give chase, but Rebecca, still behind the wheel, reaches out for my arm.

"Wait! Driving after him will be faster!"

One . . . two . . . three times the engine will not start.

My heart stops. The world stops. Nothing exists except the utter stillness of this moment.

And the turning of the key.

If the car doesn't start now, right now, with this turn, Joey will truly be gone. Killed. Frantic and afraid, he will surely dart into the high-speed traffic. My breath is ragged. I pound the dashboard with my fists; I yell at the car.

"Go, go, *go!*"

And suddenly, it does.

Lurching out of the parking lot—in stuttering slow motion—we catch up with Joey running along the freeway's edge. Pulling up beside him, we're matching his pace—the frenzied pace of the terrified—but we're still moving far more slowly than the traffic whizzing past us on our other side. Eyes wild, the whites bigger than the blue, Joey's face is streaked with tears and he's gasping for breath. Yet he's still able to scream.

"You tricked me! AGAIN! I'll never be committed to another hospital. NEVER!"

I do what I must.

As Joey stumbles and swerves, I lie.

Full of fear and out of options, I beg, *beg* him to get into the car. Leaning through the open window, I reach out to Joey, hollering over the wind and the traffic and the pounding in my ears.

"Joey, I promise, the doctor is waiting for you, but only to talk. Please, please, get in the car!"

The truth is: If the expert on suicidal behavior tells me Joey needs to be locked up, I'm locking him up. I know Joey won't care that I'm trying to save his life—because from his perspective, I'm not. But right now I can't worry about that.

Joey slows down; a sweat-lathered bronco that's run out of buck, he gets into the car.

※

A broken heart really does hurt. It's a deep, squeezing ache, and it cries. I feel it when the doctor says my son is depressed and has been for a long time.

I didn't see it.

Squeeze.

Depression—if I'd given it any thought, which I hadn't—would have looked like a curled-up ball unable to get dressed in the morning. Joey didn't look like that. Joey woke up happy (most mornings), laughed and hugged, and had friends. He loved animals and scuba diving and cooking. Sure, he'd been moody and had an eating disorder, but I thought that was teen angst. Yes, there was the arrest for possession of pot and speeding, but I thought that was just Joey acting stupid. Nothing is what I thought. It's all been signs of his depression—a depression that has now tried to kill Joey twice.

Seated across from us, on the other side of his large wooden desk, the doctor tugs on his beard, telling me that teenage depression looks different from adult depression.

"It looks like Joey," he says.

Decisions must be made about what happens next, but Joey needs to be the one to make them if whatever happens next has any chance of success. After some discussion, when Joey says he's decided to quit college and return to Maryland, I expel a long breath I don't even know I've been holding. The college dream (turned nightmare) is on hold for now. I'm filled with relief. And sadness. And dread.

Swiveling in my chair, I take a long look at Joey sitting stiffly beside me. I see more than the clenched jaw and tormented eyes. I see the pain

I missed, the mistakes I can make up for, and the tough road ahead. Reaching out, I put my hand on Joey's arm and tell him I'm sorry.

"I didn't know, Joey. So I did all the wrong things."

And then I turn back to the doctor.

"Tell me how to do things right."

"A life spent walking on eggshells is not living. You shouldn't change how you live or interact with Joey," he says. "Making concessions out of guilt or fear will only foster a sense of victimhood in Joey, but by maintaining normal expectations you'll promote strength and healing and be helping him to move forward."

Turning his attention now to Joey, the doctor continues.

"Joey, your family can support you on a path to health and happiness, but you need to do the work. Take the prescription I've given you, see a therapist, and live a healthy lifestyle. Alcohol is a depressant. You say your suicide attempt was a drunken mistake you wished you could take back once you were sober, but never forget: You can't take back dead."

◦◦◦

Joey wants to move his things out of the dorm on his own, which is fine with me; I don't think I could face being a part of the good-byes, which were, just two weeks ago, hellos.

Loading the car for the short drive to the airport, Joey hands me a "Proud SDU Mom" mug. On the surface I'm all smiley, but inside something squeezes with sadness. Neither Proud nor SDU currently apply. But Mom does. Heartsick Mom, yes. But Mom no matter what.

We've packed up so much more than sweatshirts and sheets into Joey's suitcases and boxes; they're also full of unused plans and dreams. And it hurts. So does watching Joey try to keep his head held high as we hustle to our gate. But there's no turning back.

Joey is carrying a one-way ticket to Plan B.

Delta Airlines #3487, San Diego to Washington, DC, departing 2:23 p.m.

Joey is heading home.

Verse Three

DISSONANCE

"Joey, take this time to heal and grow."

It's an entirely different perspective, being the gardener or being the rose. Where I see signs of withering and the need for a bit of nourishment, Joey sees a torrential drowning and spits out my interference. Where I work to promote his inner beauty and potential, he would rather be—and smoke—a weed. And so, our first weeks of getting settled in have been a bit prickly.

Blatantly watchful, I look for lingering signs of depression, changes in appetite, and pot smoking, and Joey resents it. Although comfortable with the perks, my independence-seeking, now-adult son is not happy with the eagle eyes and rules that come with living under his parents' roof.

Autumn arrives in Bethesda, a Maryland suburb of Washington, DC, on unsettled winds, matching the mood of our family. Joey storms around the last of the unpacked boxes crowding the hallways of our new home, blaming everyone but himself for his current situation—something Joe, Rick, and I each actually believe some of the time. Doors slam, voices rise, tears flow. I remember the doctor's warning about the pitfalls of walking on eggshells. *But if Joey is sick, shouldn't I be serving him tea and toast and fluffing his pillows rather than burdening him with work and responsibility and high expectations?* I do battle with eggshells daily.

The spiky Mohawk has disappeared, replaced by a pierced nose and peephole earlobes with a view to the side of his neck. *You look scary.*

We're covering Joey's expenses as long as he's working full-time and until he returns to college—cell phone, health insurance—but his car stays in storage. (We're paying for that, too.)

Forced to take the bus, his running response is a snarly "Fuck you." *You sound scary.* Joey has quit his therapist and his medication. He comes home from his job as a waiter smelling like pot, if he comes home at all, and an empty whiskey bottle is visible under the tan dust ruffle on his bed. *I see no evil, hear no evil, and speak no evil because I don't want to chase you away.*

I drink coffee from my "Proud SDU Mom" mug every morning, waving it around as a sign that I believe Joey can and will move forward. *A sign that I don't see you as a victim. Even though I sort of do.*

Our household is anything but harmonious. Seeking clues and truth, I check Joey's email and social media accounts regularly. (The password he gave me while applying to colleges comes in handy.) Joey doesn't know that I track his every online move. He doesn't know that I'm jarred by the dissonance of his silent words many times daily.

> I decided, well was pressured strongly, to take a year off so am back in DC with my parents until I figure out what I'm gonna do. I got arrested for marijuana and the cop thought I had crystal meth, I'll probably lose my license for six months and have to pay some fines, but its not that big of a deal. I had to get my stomach pumped for drinking too much absinthe. I kinda say fuck you mom and dad. I've gotten to the point where I am over trying to get their approval on everything, which I am happy about now. It's a lot less stressful. My parents are being shady. I have to pay for my own health insurance and car insurance and all that stuff and damn it's expensive.
> *[Email from Joey to a friend.]*

Somewhat bug-eyed by the turn of his brother's events, Rick tiptoes a straight line through the commotion of our life—no detours so far for him. Silent and strong. Or willfully invisible. I don't know how my fifteen-year-old boy is processing the struggles of his lifelong companion and role model. Does he ever worry about the sureness of his footing on his own march ahead? Does he ever wonder if there will come a time when everybody will stop yelling? *I'm sorry I'm not the mom I should be for you right now. I can barely think of anything beyond Joey. But your time will come, Rick. I promise. You'll get your mom back.*

> **I'm writing this letter to plead guilty to the charges from my August arrest. I'm not a bad person, only made some horrible decisions which I'm lucky didn't end in the death of either my best friend, another motorist, or myself. I've just turned eighteen years old and have lived with my family the whole time. I have a great family life, no alcohol or drug use, and my parents never fight. Since the incident I haven't smoked marijuana or used any other illegal substances and have found the whole experience rather eye opening to the consequences of my actions and the need to think things through.** *[Letter to the court from Joey's computer files.]*

After four months of not a lot of fun for anybody, Joey is moving out. He says he's ready to make his own life. I think what he means by that is he's ready to party without restraint. But he's an adult now. His choices, and his desire to make good choices, must come from within. My worrying and nagging sure don't work. I'm afraid for whatever comes next. And sad. But mostly I'm relieved—and I feel guilty for that.

> Me and my parents are doing ok. We're close but I'm kinda being kicked out. Well more lightly pushed out.

> They can't deal with watching me hurting myself anymore
> with drinking and drugs. Yeah I've tried a lot of new stuff
> here. Coke, ecstasy, mushrooms but I've only done them
> all once and won't do them again. I know what I'm doing.
> Kind of. Probably more than you think but less than I
> think. *[Email from Joey to a friend.]*

For months, I've sat on an uncomfortable bunch of hunches. Now, before Joey leaves, it's time to speak the unthinkable. Ambling into his room, I find Joey tossing blankets and pillows into a box. His smile fades as I launch into what he is in no mood to hear: There are addicts in our family's attic, and I don't want Joey to join them.

"You've heard this before, but this time you need to really listen. Addiction runs in our family, on both sides. Smoking pot and drinking are gambles you cannot take. You have too many relatives in various stages of recovery or active addiction to take this lightly. All of them were about your age when they started doing what you seem to think of as something everyone tries, and 'just having fun.' And they probably thought the same thing. They had no idea how un-fun things would become. They didn't know they were stepping onto a slippery slope, but you, Joey, do." I pick up a corner of a wrinkled black bedsheet, shake it out, and begin to fold. *A slippery slope. I've seen the power of addiction. And I fear it.*

Twenty-five. That's how old I was when I first gave addiction any thought. I had to. A visiting friend from my college days had the DTs (delirium tremens).

I only remember snippets of what happened after Kelly arrived in Florida. (Faint memories, thankfully, are all that remain once a nightmare retreats to the dark corner it came from.) When Joe and I picked Kelly up at the airport, we were ready for fun—newly employed newlyweds excited to show off our new life.

I don't remember exactly when I realized Kelly was crazy, but it wasn't long after we'd shown her around our tiny apartment. Maybe it was when she started squashing the speckles in the granite tabletop with her finger, mumbling about bugs. Or maybe it was when she stood in front of the birdcage, swearing back at the parrot that wasn't swearing at her. Or maybe it was when she ran out the door and through the apartment complex at the brightest point of the summer day, with spooked-horse eyes and not a lot of clothes on. No, I don't remember the moment when I knew she was crazy, but I do remember calling her mom.

"Jan, something is really wrong with Kelly."

I'd never seen addiction before. I didn't know anything about it. From my perspective, my friend had lost her mind. Kelly was the rattling top of a boiling pot ready to explode, and I wanted to escort her back to Colorado and hand her off to her mom before she did.

The first line of parental defense when dealing with a child's nightmare is to put a friendly face on the monster and shove it into the closet. That's what Kelly's mom had been doing for years. But once she heard what was going on down in Florida, she faced the monster. And she named it.

Kelly, my smart and serious college friend, was an addict.

She wasn't crazy. She was having DTs.

The vision of Kelly's mom flapping around her frenzied daughter in the tiny kitchen of their family home still haunts me. Somehow Kelly escaped. Someone called the police. And somewhere down the road she was picked up and taken to a hospital. Searching their house, Kelly's mom and I found an astonishing number of empty liquor bottles poked into handbags and sweater boxes in Kelly's bedroom closet and inside suitcases stored under her bed. Silently passing one another on the stairs, up and down, in and out, we took the empty bottles to the garbage cans behind their garage. As quickly as seemed acceptable, I left the nightmare of my friend's addiction in her mom's hands and returned home to Joe.

I wrote Kelly a letter, a real scorcher, telling her she was hurting her mom and to stop. Not long after, Kelly was released from detox. She moved back home, began an outpatient treatment program, and from afar, things seemed fine. Handled. Over.

I moved on with my life, unaware that Kelly and her mom were still in the trenches, duking it out with addiction; Kelly was lying, and drinking, and cheating the program, and her mom, doing the only thing left in her power, was trying to believe that her lying, drinking, cheating daughter wasn't.

It was a rainy day when some final straw, some new promise, was broken and Kelly's mom Let Go. She watched her daughter walk out the door—no umbrella, no money, no car—not knowing if she'd ever see her again. Weeks later the doorbell rang and Kelly stood on her mom's front porch, beaten down by whatever had happened and ready for help. She went to an inpatient addiction treatment facility, then on to a halfway house and has been living a healthy lifestyle ever since. Years later Kelly told me that she did whatever she was told because she knew if she listened to herself she was going to die.

Now, decades later, these memories are as present as the curlicues of my breath crystallizing in the winter air. I stand next to Joe, watching Joey close up the trunk of his roommate's blue sedan. He has tucked our good-luck wishes in alongside our old toaster and is ready to go. Turning, he reaches out for a hug. With my mittened hands, I hang on extra-tight. For all the worrying I've done over Joey lately, the only result is a deep crease between my eyebrows. But reason melts in the arms of my child; I'm worrying about him already. I'm worried about what happens next.

⤫

Pulling a brush through my hair as I stand before the bathroom mirror, I see that I'm smiling. *Joey has invited me to meet him downtown for an ice cream cone on this now-very-fine spring day!* I slap on some lipstick and dash out the door. Last month Rick pretended to believe me when I said Joey couldn't make it to his birthday dinner because of work. But the truth is he never bothered to return my calls. Or any calls since. *Today, though, he's called me!*

With Joey at my side, I'm beaming as I order a strawberry double-dip. I try not to notice the trembling hand that may wobble the scoop of chocolate ice cream off Joey's cone. I just want to have fun. We claim a small bistro table outside on the patio. I dole out a couple of napkins, talking happy tidbits of this and that. Joey cuts me off, voice rising.

"I've been talking to people and realize that you and Dad ripped me off. You owe me a thousand dollars since you claimed me as a dependent on last year's tax return. I want my money back. I need it. There's a cash machine down the street. Let's walk over there now."

The ice cream I'm swallowing curdles as it slides down my throat.

"But Joey, you *were* a dependent last year. We don't owe you any money. This is absurd."

As chocolate spittle and accusations of stealing fly in my face, I stand up to leave. I walk away from the barbs Joey hurls at my back, trying to appear normal, but suspect my smile looks as natural as lipstick on a corpse.

"I hate you! It's your fault I can't get ahead! Who fucking steals their kid's money? And I'm not going back to college. Not to please you. Fuck that!"

Tossing what's left of today's sweet treat and now sour illusions into the trash, I walk back to my car. There's an hour and a half left on the two-hour meter. Stunned by the dissonance between my expectations and my son's audacity, I'm unable to move any farther. I'm unable to drive. I slump forward into the steering wheel. Oh, how I long for the simpler days. Those of scabby knees and Popsicle breath and easy answers.

> It was so good to see my mom again. It means so much to her. And to me. I didn't realize how much I miss my parents. They are so supportive of me and it's really nice to have that. I feel sad cuz I feel like I'm letting them down you know? I just want to make them proud and I'm not. Someday I WILL. I can never be good to anyone I love unless I am good to myself. I have gone from being a spoiled little shit, who had everything, to someone who couldn't support anyone other than myself and that's not good enough for me. *[Email from Joey to a friend.]*

When Joey shows up at the back door, a few brown leaves from the walnut tree drift in behind him. A blotchy rash covers the parts of Joey not covered by his T-shirt, but he doesn't want to talk about that so I give him a hug and pretend nonchalance at this rare visit.

Pulling a stool up to the kitchen counter, Joey leans forward.

"Mom, I need twelve hundred dollars. I quit my job at the restaurant. You wouldn't believe the bad stuff going down over there. I'm starting a new job in a few days, but I need money to pay my rent and bills until I get my first paycheck."

Setting aside the meatballs I've been preparing for dinner, I look at my watch. Rick will be home from school shortly; this little discussion will need to be quick.

"Okay, Joey, since you have a new job lined up, I'll loan you the money. But. Don't ever ask for money again. You need to learn from this and be prepared for when things don't go quite right. You cannot expect to be rescued. This is not a gift. I expect to be paid back on a schedule and on time—and this will include the twenty-eight hundred dollars you already owe us for your health insurance since moving out." Looking at his eager-to-please face, I see, and seize, an opportunity. "I'll loan you this money only if you remove whatever it is that's holding open the huge holes in your earlobes."

You want money. I want you to look less scary. Win, win.

Moving into the living room, we sit down, stretch out our legs, and giggle at our sneaker collisions on the shared yellow tuffet. Together we map out Joey's financial situation—he owes thousands of dollars in past-due bills and overdrawn accounts, but promises he will get and stay on top of things now—and then we gab. About nothing and everything. A pretty darn good moment.

When Rick and Joe get home, I tell them how masterfully I handled the situation. They both look at me like I'm an idiot. It does seem stupid to have loaned Joey all that money now that I see the transaction through less befuddled eyes.

Mother's Day. Not even a phone call from Joey.

Holes—the things that aren't—are every bit as real as mountains—and so, what *isn't* happening is every bit as real, and significant, as what *is*. The phone that doesn't ring, the missed birthdays and holidays, the no-show coffee dates, the end of the pretense of returning to college—these are the holes. The convoluted lies and excuses, the lost jobs, and the reports of unremitting disasters at Joey's apartment—alcohol poisoning, shattered glass and gushing blood, emergency rescues, and an arrest—well, these are the mountains.

I don't know why Joey was arrested, but I go to the courthouse to show him he's not alone. A show of support. And hope. Joe would be here too, but he has to work. As I wait in the slowly moving line to be scanned for concealed knives, guns, and nunchucks, I'm caught between two giants wearing black leather, spikes, and razor-edged irritation. I've never been in a courthouse before (other than to get my marriage license, but that must have been at the happy entrance) and I feel ridiculous in my Petal Pink lipstick and matching handbag.

When I find Joey slouched on a bench in a crowded waiting room, I'm so relieved. He looks up, and I smile. But his face contorts as he leaps to his feet; on the verge, it appears, of vomiting out a rabid beast.

"What the fuck are you doing here? Go away. This is some stupid fucking charge by a stupid fucking cop. I don't need you here fucking things up. I don't fucking want you here. Leave me alone."

So, that's what I do.

Joe, Rick, and I have just finished dinner and are digging into dessert when Joey stops by the house with a bouquet of fall flowers and an apology.

"I'm sorry, Mom. I was stressed out," he says. "Not everybody has a parent who would show up in court like that. I realize that. So thanks."

"Well, what happened today?" I ask. I don't ask about the crime.

"The judge put me on probation. Drug education and community service shit. *Asshole*. But he can't stop me from smoking pot. I love pot, will always smoke pot, and no one can stop me."

"Joey," I sigh.

"Have you ever tried it? You should. Everyone should."

I tell Joey I think his life is out of control and that he needs help.

"Maybe a twelve-step or addiction treatment program," Joe adds, wiping a few cake crumbs from his lips with his napkin. Eyes averted.

There it is. The thing Joe and I have whispered about between ourselves but have been afraid to say out loud to our son.

"Yes, I need help!" Joey hollers. "What kind of parents are you? You won't give me the car I earned, you won't pay for me to go to college, and you won't give me money when I'm having tough times. How am I supposed to be able to afford to live on my crappy income in this crappy town? Work and more work, that's my life, and I have no hope of ever getting ahead because you never help me out. Parents who love their kids help their kids. I need real help, not the sort of shit you're talking about. Addiction treatment shit. Fuck you. I'll just keep getting help from the people who really care about me—my friends. I don't need or want your kind of help, which is useless. How dare you accuse me of having any kind of problem? YOU are my problem."

When I call around to some of Joey's old friends, I hear that I'm overreacting.

"Everybody our age tries drugs. Unless it involves needles or crack, it's not something to be worried about." I don't believe them. I continue to worry.

⁓

Today, I really miss my own mom.

Of three siblings, I'm the only girl, sandwiched two and a half years on either side between Richard, the eldest, and David, the goofiest. Growing up in Golden Valley, Minnesota, we lived in a yellow colonial-style house with black shutters at the windows and a milk box on the front porch, and filled our days with riding bikes and sledding and playing in the woods, or pelting one another with icy snowballs and giving Mom gray hair (and Dad no hair).

During high school we still got along well enough—we weren't best buddies but we could stand to be in the same room together—and during college we would catch up around the kitchen table when we migrated home for holidays and summers. But once our grown-up lives took shape, as we scattered across the country and our trips back home were less synchronized, sibling updates fell to Mom and Dad in weekly calls, with news, security and love relayed from the phone nearest the well-worn La-Z-Boy in the den. Comfort Central.

Mom, I need you. But I don't want to worry you. Please pick up the phone and call me right now.

Solid Midwestern folks; my dad is a doctor and my mom is a nurse. Sometime in the early 1950s they met on the ward of a county hospital in Saint Paul, Minnesota. Mom in her starched white uniform, nursing cap, and cat glasses. Dad in his resident jacket with a stethoscope hanging from his neck. Someone proposed to someone else while holding hands on a long walk and they've been happily married ever since. My parents' weekly routine includes a lot of togetherness; grocery shopping, brisk hikes, and turns at the churches of their different denominations. Dad mows the grass, keeps Mom's car topped off with gas, and irons his own shirts now that her hands are crippled with arthritis. Mom is tiny; I can rest my chin on her curly white head. A little bird, she bakes pies and cookies for Dad (a plumper bird), and fusses over him if he doesn't wear a hat to protect his bald head. My parents see the world as they treat the world: gently.

My world isn't feeling very gentle right now.

Mom, call me.

⁓

Hysteria becomes begging, which becomes scheming, which becomes anger, which becomes a dial tone. Joey hangs up because Joe refuses to drop off a car so he can drive to his girlfriend's house and save her from a dose of bad cocaine and certain death. He didn't care for Joe's suggestion that Joey call 911. The phone rings again within minutes, but this time Joey is crying.

"Dad, help me. Please, Dad, come get me."

Joe is out the door in five seconds.

Returning a short while later, Joe shoots me a warning look as he shakes off his boots and holds the door open for Joey. My son steps in from the dark, pale and twitching. He zooms through the kitchen and down the hall, in and out of rooms, choking on tears and fears and garbled words about cocaine. Joe and I follow around after him, trying to soothe the wild beast; somehow, eventually, after whatever he's on wears off, we wait and listen. Joey lies down in his old bedroom, murmuring the words we've been waiting to hear.

"I need help. I need addiction treatment. I can't do this anymore." And he falls asleep.

Sadness leaks onto my pillow until I'm overcome with exhaustion. But then, drawn from a fitful sleep, I tiptoe through the house to check on Joey before dawn. He's in the TV room, sitting in near darkness, propped up next to his girlfriend, Julianne, on our green sofa.

Where did she come from?

Neither of them moves, not even a bit, although their expressions become slightly amused, as though I'm some freaky apparition that magically appeared for their viewing pleasure. I don't know what's going on, but it feels smarmy. This doesn't match up with what happened here earlier this night.

"Both of you, get out."

They do. They stand up and float right out the door. Looking around, I notice a stain on the beige carpet. It looks like blood. *What went on here during the night?* Holding the edge of the coffee table for balance, I crouch down to touch the ruby wetness, and then slowly bring it to my nose. Not blood. *Wine.*

Growling now, I shake my head, trying to free my mind of the ugliness snaking into my thoughts. How dare Joey bring his scary world into our life and our home—his drugs, his drinking, his darling little dealer, and whatever that drama was that happened last night?

Furious, I slam my way through the rest of the morning, slamming doors and drawers and cabinets. I slam waffles into the toaster and then onto Rick's plate (who then eats them in silence). Once Rick leaves for school I head to the garage, slam my car into reverse, and take my fury to Joey.

At Joey's apartment, a long-haired stranger opens the door, a silent zombie who shuffles off to flop on the saggy black sofa in the middle of the room, leaving me to stand at the entrance. Not sure what to do,

I stay where I am, taking a look around. The blinds are drawn against the morning light but I can see dried blood and other crud all over the carpet and walls. I presume the widely splattered blood stains are from the mysterious broken sliding-glass-door incident. Amidst crumpled bits of trash and dirty dishes, a Christmas tree stands in the corner, decorated with silver garlands and a few ornaments from Joey's childhood. More than the decrepitude of this place where Joey lives, it's the tree—Joey's attempt at re-creating fond memories—that makes me want to cry.

Stepping farther into the apartment, I tap on Joey's door. No response. I'm not at all sure I want to see whatever's in there. But I have some yelling to do. So, I turn the grimy knob with two fingers and slowly push my way in.

Fully dressed (minus a sneaker), Joey is sprawled on his back across his bed. His long legs are twisted in the less-than-fresh-looking sheets. His eyes are closed, he's breathing heavily. One arm is bent over his forehead, the other dangles above an empty wine bottle on the floor.

"Joey," I whisper softly. Not to rouse him, but to see if it's safe to snoop without getting caught. Not an eyelash flickers. The small room smells of ashtrays, recently smoked pot, and things unwashed; I hold the back of my hand to my nose. Three of the walls are the color of a cigarette filter after a few puffs, and the wall over his bed is spray-painted with mostly black graffiti. Bongs, baggies, and cigarette butts litter the carpet between stiff-looking socks and mildewed towels, and the printer from college sits in one corner gathering dust while robust marijuana plants stand tall in another.

Stepping over some junk, I reach for his backpack. There's another empty wine bottle and a corkscrew inside. I'm pretty sure these came from the room where Joe and I keep our liquor locked up—a recent precaution in case Joey ever came over. I guess he found a way in. If his room wasn't so filthy, I might allow myself to crumple up on the floor and cry until tomorrow. Instead, I call out Joey's name, this time loud and sharp.

Like rusty old hinges, his eyes slowly creak open, get a little stuck, close, and creak back open. Merely a crack. He remains deathly still. And silent. I'm fairly certain Joey's not aware I'm here, but I yell at him anyway. I let go of my fury over last night's drama, drugs, and deceit. I feel a little better, but I'm not quite done.

"Take a look at your life, at this mess, at everything you are throwing away. Get a grip. Grow up. Be responsible. Take control. Make something of yourself, Joey. Make a life you can be proud of. Oh, and, one more thing. I love you. Don't ever forget that."

✑

"How about a bike?" Joe asks me.

"No. I can picture Joey riding around in traffic while high or drunk. How about if we reduce his debt?" I reply.

"I don't think so. That would send the wrong message and set a bad precedent. An iPod?"

"He'd sell it for drug money."

Finally Joe and I decide to give Joey a bathrobe for Christmas. Boring yet safe. And a handmade certificate decorated with yellow smiley faces— admission to Havenwood Addiction Treatment Center (redeemable at any time), not at all sure how Joey will respond. Since he was wigged out last week when he admitted to needing help, we are relieved when he says he will use it.

"I think my life is a little out of control."

I'm so happy I can hardly stand it. I've already talked to the Havenwood folks up in Minnesota so I know there will be space available for Joey in a few weeks. I whip out my list and start preparations. I buy Joey's airplane ticket and move $25,000 of his college funds into our checking account to pay for the first month of addiction treatment. With three days to go and everything lined up to go except Joey, I set out to track him down— he hasn't answered any of my calls since Christmas—and find him at the restaurant where he works. When Joey says he's not going to Havenwood after all, I crumble. A snuffling, begging mess. Joey cries a little too, wrapping his arms around me and patting me on the back.

"I'm so sorry for everything, Mom. But everything will be okay now. I'll go. I'll go."

A dollop of something sweet floating in our sour pot.

Almost a year to the day after he moved out of our house, Joey moves back home. For one night. It's another cold January day of packing up boxes, but this time around my emotions aren't mixed. When I arrive at Joey's apartment, the only indication he's even thought about moving is the absence of his marijuana crop. I don't care where it went. I only care that it's gone. Joey is high. Hazy and weird, he keeps negotiating to get rid of me. *Fat chance.* He mentions wanting to break up with Julianne.

"We do too many bad things together."

The breaking up part is a bit of good news and I hang onto that.

Chucking Joey's jumbled bundles of stuff into the back of my SUV, I'm startled by the appearance of a husky, dark-haired young man at my side. But he's smiling, asking if I'm Joey's mom and if Joey is upstairs.

"Yes and yes! He's in the apartment, packing; the door is open," I say, smiling back, and then get back to my chucking. Moments later I hear loud curses and thumping. Whirling around, I see Joey shoving The Smiler down the stairs from his second floor apartment. Then Joey is screaming at me, right up in my face.

"Mind your own fucking business! That guy is a dealer who wants to kill me and you go fucking let him into my house? You have no fucking idea what you are doing! You are crazy!" Only when Joey storms away do I dare move. I lean into my car, rearranging the mess into a different mess. Swallow hard. Blink hard. Try to focus on the goal.

By the time we dump Joey's belongings in our basement, it's already dark, Joe is home from work, and we enter a new moon of madness. Looking over the Havenwood packing list—no cell phone, no iPod, no laptop, nothing sharp—Joey balks.

"No fucking way. What the hell are you getting me into?" Then he calls Julianne and walks out the door. Joe steps out after him.

"Don't be too late! You've got laundry and packing to do! And you need to wake up early!"

As though we let Joey leave. We know Joey is leaving whether we let him leave or not. What we don't know is if he'll come back.

Joe and I decide to poke around in Joey's things. We find glass bongs and metal pipes, a small scale, a rectangular mirror, and other, unidentifiable paraphernalia. Now what do we do? If we throw it all away,

Joey will notice—assuming he returns tonight—sabotaging the goal for tomorrow. If we confront him, we'll need to draw some kind of line in the shifting sand. That will likely send him right back out the door. My vote is to wait until he's gone and then throw it all away.

"Nope, I'm done being held hostage," Joe says.

When Joey stumbles through the back door, bumps off the wall, and spins around in our direction, Joe and I are waiting for him—grim-faced, barefoot, and wearing our PJs. Joey's drug supplies are spread out on the kitchen counter.

"What the fuck? You went through my shit? That's my personal property. You fucking violated my rights!" Red-faced and weaving, he fumbles around with the paraphernalia, trying to stuff it all into the front of his shirt. "You can't take these! I bought them. I'm going to hide them where you'll never fucking find them!" Joey barrels back out into the night, curdling my blood with his fury.

⌘

Tossing and turning, I can't sleep. I sneak out of bed and down the hall, avoiding the squeaky floorboard just inside my study, and ease the door closed behind me. Without turning on the lamp, I burrow into the cushions of my overstuffed chair. Joey is banging around downstairs—high, agitated, and unpredictable. Over the years I have felt afraid *for* Joey. But I've never felt afraid *of* him. Until tonight. Tonight, I am both. So here I sit, quietly sewing one bump and thump and slam into the next with the stitch of my breathing. Maybe somehow my vigil will carry him all the way to sunrise. Somehow keep him from lighting up or sneaking out or running away. Joey needs to be here come daylight; he's got a flight to catch. So, I take a breath. I hold it as I wait for the next bump. I breathe.

And I think.

Sometime between the first hint of a whisker and the nudge from the nest, Joey crossed an invisible line—a line where experimentation became addiction. And dalliance became disease. He was a kid when he started down the path that brought him here to this night—just a kid when he made the choices that turned out to be bad choices, influenced by feelings and pressures more powerful than his tender young self could withstand. Besieged by music, movies, magazines, and malls, Joey was lured in.

"Drugs, drinking, party! A carefree life! A dream life! A pain-free life! Sign in blood here."

Such intoxicating enticements. (Don't bother to read the fine print.)

An addict is a pea-in-the-pod who spoils the party, shunned by the very same peers who had passed the poisoned apple, as well as by those who slyly winked or looked the other way.

"This is so unexpected, so shocking."

"What a disgrace."

"What a mess."

The world of addiction is a murky place, but one thing is crystal clear: Millions of people choose to take a first drink or first drug—and a second and a third and a hundredth—yet they don't all become addicts. And, of those who do become addicts, not one of them chooses to. People may choose to use, but they do not choose to lose. Something else does the choosing when a user becomes an addict.

When I was in high school and college, I partied a lot. I slugged down more Boone's Farm and Schlitz and peach schnapps than I care to admit. I never gave a thought to the risk. Not once. If I had, I would've thought addiction only happened to other people. Seriously flawed and weak people. I didn't know the fun I was having was fun by pure luck. I didn't know there were others in the family who would be taken down by the drink. I didn't know that when I chose to drink, the drink could just as easily have chosen *me.*

Everyone I know eats donuts and cookies and candy-store sweets. Some, but not all, become diabetic or are haunted by visions of sugarplums or land on the scale between chubby and obese. Is slow-torture-by-donut a choice? What makes someone susceptible to heart disease or multiple sclerosis? What makes someone good at math, or stink at drawing, or hate the taste of anchovies, or favor the color blue? What makes one shy, one gregarious, or one like toy cars more than teddy bears before the age of two? I think we're born with a mix of ingredients and there are some things about which we have no choice.

So, what turns a user into an addict? I don't know, but I'm sitting here in the dark, hiding from my nineteen-year-old son who is one. Some inner turmoil may have drawn Joey to experiment with drugs and drink, but his inner turmoil did not make him an addict. Something else did.

Morning is here. And so is Joey. Bleary-eyed and subdued, he says he's ready to go to the airport and has a bulging suitcase to prove it. He will be flying alone; Joey needs to feel he's *going* to addiction treatment rather than being *taken*. If disaster is averted over the next several hours, it will probably be simply because we've made sure he has no money.

I should feel happy this morning now that there's a glimmer of light at the end of Joey's tunnel. Instead, I have mixed feelings. Much, I suppose, like a mother learning of a new treatment option for her child's rapidly spreading cancer.

It may be good news, but only relatively speaking.

Verse Four

SOMETHING CRAZY-BAD

Like mamas everywhere, I discovered the power of the bond created during pregnancy—that intimate nine-month love affair between two souls. A phantom connection, unaffected by the passage of years or a long stretch of miles, mysteriously wanders the invisible world, searching for tears and for fears and for when things are not quite right, and then relays that information back to home base. I can read a full day's story on the faces of my children without a word passing between us. I've awakened in the night, waiting for the groggy call that floats my way moments later. And I can tell when one of my boys is smiling just by looking at the back of his head. The force of this bond sends moms of all species into dive-bombs or snarling rages to protect their young, and into frenzied action or keening grief for a cub gone missing.

I've been surprised over and over by the power of this stuff of motherhood. It bloomed from some unknown place deep within me, literally overnight, and is virtually indestructible.

But sometimes I don't want it, because it hurts too much.

The house grows quiet once Joe and Joey leave for the airport and Rick leaves for school. I pull on my jacket and step outside, bracing myself against the freezing-cold air. For once in my life I'm wishing for snow;

I wish there were tracks to help me find the bongs Joey hid out here last night. I wander the crunchy lawn without direction. Picking up a stick, I poke at the rotted center of an old tree stump and around the fence posts. On my knees, I burrow into a tangle of twiggy honeysuckle legs, raking my gloved fingers through frosty brown leaves. I don't find what I'm looking for, but do see a scattering of empty bottles a short toss into the neighbor's yard; some of last night's racket was probably Joey scuttling out the door with even more things that needed to be erased in the darkness.

Returning to the house, I hang my jacket on the hook by the back door and survey the scraps of Joey's life abandoned in the haste of his retreat. Stepping through the ruins, I pick up pieces here and there, trying to consolidate the mess disgorged across our home without looking too closely, but the scraps of Joey's life and dreams bring me to my knees. *To my knees.*

The heap of college textbooks, never opened; the yellow pencils, never sharpened; the tent, camp stove, fishing poles, and fly-tying feathers; the ski pants and dress pants; the one scuffed-up dress shoe (where's the other?). The neat little stack of "I Love You" cards he received in the mail from his mom every week for the past year. *He didn't throw them away.*

And the photos. Joey, bright-eyed, baby-toothed, and beaming, holding high his first trout. Joey showing his brother how to cast a rod. Joey in the Alps. Joey scuba diving in Thailand. Joey, posing all over the place with his dad and his brother and me, and smiling. *Where did Joey's smiles and dreams go?* I find a hole cut into the side of his discarded mattress, semiconcealed by the square of fabric still hinged in place. I open the little access hatch, afraid I'll find something illicit hoarded away, but it's empty. Just like me.

The doorbell rings. Craig, Joey's old roommate, stands on the stoop. He's medium in every way: height, hair color, looks. I've met Craig before and wondered why he hangs around Joey, who's ten years his junior—and why Joey hangs out with someone so creepy and insincere. I open the door.

"Good morning! I'm so sorry to bother you today of all days. I heard Joey is off to get the help he so desperately needs, but he left owing me $700. I'm hoping you will find it in your heart to help me out and make things right."

"Make things right." This from someone who didn't seek me out to make things right when Joey was the one needing help.

"Well, Craig. I'm not paying you a penny. Not only is this not my problem, I have every reason to believe this is a drug debt. So, take this issue up with your friend Joey, the drug addict. If you hang out in the gutters, you're gonna get wet. So don't act surprised and expect innocent bystanders to step in and dry you off."

I can almost hear the greasy gears of his mind trying to crank out words that might squeeze a little something out of me yet. Craig stretches his elastic smile wider.

"Ma'am, I don't do drugs. But Joey, he was really into cocaine and Percocet. He was always drinking and doing drugs at work, even sneaking out back to do mushrooms with his girlfriend. Joey has some really bad friends. And he owes a lot of money to a lot of people. So, you'd better be careful."

Have I just been threatened? My neck prickles.

If Craig ever reappears, we must pretend no one is home. I need to warn Rick.

Closing the door, I lean my forehead against the icy pane and shut my eyes, the morning events scuttling around in my brain. Unwelcome attic dwellers looking for cover. When the phone rings, I jump. And run. Not so much to answer it as to make it stop. It's Joey; he's made it to Havenwood. He didn't run away, and it doesn't sound like he got drunk on the plane. I heave a huge sigh. Joey is now on the road to recovery—though he's not at peace with it yet.

Hysterical is more like it. High-pitched and breathless, Joey rips everything and everyone he's encountered today to shreds.

"So you'd better hurry up and get me out of here before something bad happens!"

I'm shaken. Not by Joey's wild complaints, but by his wild desperation. Not only is Joey not sweetly surrendering; he's trying to manipulate an exit. Shamelessly tugging on the "Mommy, I'm not safe" strings even though the choice to walk in—and walk out—is his. As I'm warming a late-morning cup of coffee in the microwave, the phone rings again. This time it's Ivan, another friend of Joey's.

"I heard Joey's gone into treatment. He's a good guy underneath it all, but is deep into some really bad stuff. Especially cocaine." I sit down in the dining room as Ivan tells me about my son.

"Joey doesn't do anything in moderation. I tried to get him to slow down but finally had to stop seeing him. I couldn't watch Joey killing himself anymore."

"Havenwood is definitely where Joey belongs," I say.

"Julianne is bad news," Ivan continues. "And Craig is big trouble—a drug user, a dealer, and a felon. He's on the run from a car theft conviction. I admit, I drink and smoke pot a lot, but don't do the hard stuff. It ruins lives." Ivan pauses. "Look at Joey. He had such a good life, so much opportunity. He could've gone to college, and he threw it all away."

The unexpected conversations with Ivan and Craig light a fire inside me. A blazing fear, yes. But also a burning desire for the truth. Joey is more lost than I imagined. It's time to pull my head out of the sand and take a look around. I need to know the *whole* truth if I'm going to go head-to-head with Joey's addiction.

Within the hour, I sit in my car with Sherri, Joey's as-of-yesterday abandoned roommate. She's just hopped inside, bringing along some chilly air, but I can already feel the sun streaming through the windshield and across our laps. Sherri rakes her fingers through her long, strawberry-blond hair and tells me the story she knows. The Joey she knows.

"Joey was stealing from me a lot; once he even took my rent money from my dresser. I was afraid of the friends he always had hanging around. And Joey was forever late paying the rent, making trouble with the landlord. No matter how much he worked, he never had any money."

Joey had lost a lot of friends over the past months, the once loveable guy swapped out with someone weird and unpredictable. And being Joey's friend had become scary. He owed a lot of money to a lot of people—over $5,000 to just one of them—and those people had been harassing Joey's friends.

"Joey was fired for drinking on the job a few months ago, but he was telling everyone he quit," Sherri says. "He was seriously into cocaine, drinking, and smoking pot; I never saw him go a day without using.

Using. Buying. Selling. That was Joey's whole life." She confirms my worst fears. "Remember the time Joey borrowed your car to move furniture for me? He was lying. He needed the car for a drug deal. Somebody stole drugs from somebody and Joey ended up getting pistol-whipped that night." Sherri is pulling back my blinders, and I'm not sure I want to look. "One night I came home and found the sliding glass door shattered. There was broken glass and big puddles of blood everywhere. Joey wouldn't tell me what happened, but I could tell it was something crazy bad."

Julianne is an addict; Craig got Joey started on cocaine and who-knows-what-else; and the guy who freaked Joey out on moving day is a crackhead known for having stabbed someone. These are the people in Joey's world.

And these are the people Joey brought into my world.

Climbing out of the car, Sherri hands me a piece of paper she's been twisting; a note Joey left in her room, after a binge not long ago, next to a packet of cocaine.

"The note asked me to get rid of the cocaine, so I flushed it down the toilet. Joey was terrified that he'd overdosed. He'd done a massive amount of cocaine that night. Joey had so many bad nights. So many times he said he would never do cocaine again. But he always did. The next morning, Joey wanted his cocaine back. When he found out it was gone, that I'd flushed it, I was afraid."

Sherri, I had a bad night. I'm sorry I did it again after I promised I wouldn't. I dunno why I did. Anyways, I did at least 10g myself...feel like I'm gonna die and think I free-based with my friend cuz there's a burned spoon in my room. Take a look at this and tell me what it is and if it's good or not and how do I feel better? Oh, and this is the remainder of a ball the guy gave me to get me through the morning...doesn't freaking help at all! I need more weed! Screw blow!

Joey's girlfriend is next on my calling card. She's waiting for me when I walk into the local Starbucks. Brown eyes, pretty smile. Very, very thin. Still reverberating inside my head is the drumbeat I've heard all day—*Julianne is trouble*. I get that. But I can't help feeling sorry for her too.

She's yet another tragedy.

She's another mother's Joey.

As we stand in line to order coffee, part of me (the part that doesn't hate her) wants to give Julianne a hug and tell her to run—from drugs, from Joey, from the whole hideous lifestyle. But I don't. I can't. I only have the energy to focus on one mess: my son. And I only have energy to listen.

"Joey was already bad off when I met him," Julianne begins. Her voice is smoker-husky. "Drinking every night to get drunk, smoking a lot of pot. Taking Benadryl—he told me you noticed the rash he got from that; it was all over his body. Joey gets mean when he's drunk. And he's an embarrassment."

Julianne tells me about the night of the broken sliding-glass-door incident. Drunk and high after a night of partying, Joey couldn't find the key to his apartment. While she waited out front, Joey went around back, climbed onto his balcony on the second floor, and threw a patio chair through the glass door and into his apartment. His solution to the problem of how to get in.

Horrified yet giggling, Joey scooped up Julianne to carry her over the shattered glass. Two steps in, they toppled over; Joey landed on top of her, and a long shard of glass impaled her inner arm. With her blood spurting in great arcs, they ran around the apartment, afraid to call 911 for fear of getting in trouble. But then they became more afraid of what would happen if they didn't call for help. Joey was belligerent with the paramedics and police. He got a citation for a bong left out on the coffee table; but if his bedroom door hadn't been closed off from view, his situation would have gotten much worse.

Julianne's arm rests on the square table between us. The sleeve of her navy blue sweater is pushed up and I see the gouged-out dent on her inner arm that led to a blood transfusion and thirty-eight stitches.

"Joey was always borrowing money from everyone. And he never paid them back. Once he sort of paid me back the rent money I loaned him, but the check bounced. He never had enough money to do anything fun." Julianne leans back from the table, piercing me with her eyes. "You know, you set him up for his crappy life. You didn't let him go to college or have his car. Joey was always telling anyone who'd listen that his parents didn't love him and treated him bad. Joey didn't want to go to Havenwood, but because of your tears he pretended he did. He never intended to actually go, but went on a crazy bender in case you forced him."

&

I feel like I've been dreaming while I'm awake, only it's been a nightmare—and the nightmare isn't a dream. Unable to sleep last night, I don't think I'll be able to sleep tonight either. My worry that Joey wouldn't make it through the night last night is dwarfed by fear that Joey won't make it through his life.

Determined to know everything there is to know about Joey's sordid life, once the dishes are washed and Joe and Rick have gone to bed, I open Joey's laptop—the one we gave him for college—discarded, along with everything else he owns, downstairs. What I find, mostly, is photos. Photos of a pasty-faced, bleary-eyed Joey sucking from bongs and pipes and funnels, photos of bags and bags and bags of marijuana spread out across his coffee table, and photos of stacks and stacks of hundred-dollar bills.

Is there a word for an already broken heart that gets broken some more?

How am I supposed to make it from dusk to dawn (and dawn to dusk) knowing now, picturing the damage that my son has been inflicting on his body and soul? The fuzzy notions I had of Joey's drug-addled life are no longer fuzzy *or* notions. I should feel unburdened, having shed my blinders. But I don't. Sheer terror must weigh more than ignorance.

My one wish is that my boys are happy and healthy and good. Really, that's all any mom ever wants. But Joey has strayed far, far off that most wished-for course. He's strayed into a world I know little—and can do little—about. This thing that's gotten hold of my son is strong. Maybe even stronger than he is. Can he fight addiction? Can he survive if he cannot?

Can I?

The damn bond of motherhood hurts.

MORE THAN A BLIP

A few weeks ago, when Joey packed his bag for Havenwood, I already had one of my own packed for an Operation Smile mission to Nicaragua. I was going to photograph children undergoing cleft surgeries, just as I'd done in Dharamsala, India. But my suitcase never left the corner of my bedroom; when Joey went to Havenwood, I abandoned my trip. Now, rolling the suitcase out of its long-term parking spot and heaving it onto the bed, I pull out all things light-weight and short-sleeved. In their place, I fold wool sweaters and turtlenecks and other frigid-Minnesota gear; Havenwood's family program is coming up.

I know a few people who've gone to rehab, and they've been fine ever since—that's pretty much all I know about addiction treatment. From that, I take hope: Joey will be in and out of Havenwood in twenty-eight days, all this trauma nothing more than a little growing-pain blip. Like my own little growing-pain blip.

In moving up to high school from middle school, I cast off my little-girl dorkiness onto my purple shag smiley-face rug and welcomed the new me: a thirteen-year-old grownup. It was not a graceful transition. I started to paint frosted streaks of bright blue eye shadow across my lids and wore a tan that came from a can. I was caught holding a cigarette in the haze of the unsanctioned smokers' bathroom and was suspended from school for three days. I listened to David Bowie, carrying around my red radio-ball on a chain. I smoked pot and drank whatever liquor my thirteen-year-old friends could steal from their parents and bring to our clandestine parties. And once, I told my dad to "fuck off," right up in his face. So bold for someone wearing braided pigtails, bell-bottoms, and braces. One night I arrived home drunk and stumbled around in the yard. By the next morning it had been arranged for me to finish the school year down in Kansas with my dad's sister and her family. Several months later I moved back into my old bedroom, all the drama nothing more than a little growing-pain blip. *It will be the same way with Joey.*

Contemporary brick with lots of big windows and light, Havenwood Addiction Treatment Center isn't too far from the heart of downtown Spirit Lake, Minnesota, yet it's in the middle of nowhere. It's a long walk for anyone looking for trouble, especially with deep snow and zero-degree weather. I'm happy about that. Joey is in the youth addiction program, so everyone gathered in the small classroom with Joe and me are parents.

A lot of sad-looking parents. In looking around, I see myself. Quivering breaths suddenly escape my lips even though I try hard to stop them. I feel a gentle pat on my arm; it's another mother. In this room, the pain behind our untold stories is understood. Deep fear, high hopes, endless love. We have nothing in common and everything in common. A roomful of strangers hoping to learn the magic trick or word that will bring a stray child back within reach.

I'm surprised to discover the family program is for us, the parents. Instead of focusing on ways to get and keep Joey in recovery—he's busy learning that for himself—Joe and I learn ways to cope. And we learn that addiction is a brain disease brought on by a constellation of genetic, psychological, social, and behavioral factors.

Oh, thank God this is not our fault.

"You didn't cause it, you can't cure it, and you can't control it. But it can be controlled—by the addict. There's no easy way out, but a lifetime of recovery is very attainable and your children are learning the tools for success. Temptation is inevitable. But relapse is not."

We hear a lot about enabling. We're not supposed to do anything that makes it easy for an addict to be an addict. Like loaning money. Or paying bills. Or un-sticking sticky wickets. Or listening to lies.

I get it.

Joey's future is in Joey's hands; he's got work to do and I need to stay out of his way.

My enabling must stop.

Our parent group is joined by two young addicts nearing the end of their treatment; I don't know their names. Pimply Cherub is the son of a minister. It was just a few years ago, as a young teen, that a friend introduced him to cocaine. Shaved Head is seventeen years old now, but he was only eight when his dad gave him his first drink. This is his third time trying to get a grab on recovery. For an hour or so these boys tell the tales of their downward spirals. Spirals they were very successful in manipulating others to help them spiral down further. I sniffle, but not alone.

"Tough love means never cleaning up an addict's vomit; let him face and clean up his own mess in the morning. If you really want to help your kids, stop the enabling. Stop helping to kill them," says Pimply Cherub.

"Addicts working on their recovery want real help; they don't want to avoid it. But addicts still hanging onto addiction do not. And they hate programs like this because what people like you learn here makes hanging onto their addiction much harder," adds Shaved Head.

I need to love Joey enough to love him tough.

⁓

"I'm addicted to cocaine and alcohol but I'm not addicted to pot. I love pot and will never quit smoking it." Joey paces around our tight knot of chairs like a caged porcupine—prickly and poised for attack— so Joe and I handle him carefully. Joey is not happy with Havenwood's recommendation that he continue addiction treatment for another four months. He is focused on reuniting with Julianne; it seems they've both forgotten they didn't really like each other that much. Our desperation barely concealed behind forced smiles, Joe and I toss out options. Halfway house. "Sober College." Anything to keep Joey away from the miserable life he's got on pause back home. Anything to give recovery another day to sink in. Since he still thinks he can smoke pot, he clearly needs it.

"You, and only you, will be with you every day of your life. Right now you need to make decisions for you and your future alone, decisions that will leave you whole and happy. Your dad and I have also made a decision; we've decided that if you choose to discontinue addiction treatment, you'll also be choosing to forfeit your plane ticket back home."

Joey agrees to go to the halfway house simply, I think, because he has nowhere else to go.

I had thought the hard part of battling addiction would be the first twenty-eight days, but I now understand the enormity of what will be a lifelong commitment. I now understand the hard part will be the rest of Joey's life. And I understand that Joey does not yet understand this.

Addiction is more than a blip. Addiction is forever. It can be controlled by following a treatment plan, as with any other serious disease, but there is no cure. It can't simply be stuffed back in the bottle or under the rug. It's a chronic disease and relapse is likely—because doing what is needed to stay in recovery forever happens one day at a time and is damn hard work.

Twenty-eight isn't a magic number; it doesn't even have anything to do with optimum results. Instead, the twenty-eight-day stint typical of most addiction treatment facilities is determined by what insurance companies will cover. As I listen to the parents seated around me, most of whom are scrambling to cash in stock or raid retirement pensions, it seems that getting insurance coverage for addiction treatment is as arbitrary as the number of days insurance companies have deemed sufficient for getting well. Our medical insurance will pay exactly zero dollars of Joey's $25,000 bill for twenty-eight days of treatment at Havenwood. When Joey moves to the halfway house it will cost far less, but still, it's going to be a whopping $4,600 a month. Joe and I are fortunate to be able to pay for this—at least for a while. My guess is that most addicts don't get the help they need.

As Joe maneuvers the car through slick curves and snowbanks and heads toward the airport, I give Rick a call. He's only half-listening; his other half is playing a video game. From reading between grunts, it seems he's content eating microwaved frozen empanadas for dinner and using his sleeve as a napkin. But I'm sad he's home alone.

I'm keenly aware of all the times I've abandoned him to deal with Joey. Rick's a junior in high school, independent, and he's never gotten into any trouble, but I want to be there with him. I want to read his face when he tells me about the physics test he took at school and the cranky customer he encountered at his after-school job at the greenhouse. I want to play a game of cards or two and talk about the latest movies. *I want to share the moments that will never pass by again.* I fear that in trying to reel in one son, I might be throwing out the other. *But what can I do?*

⁂

Grabbing onto a fence rail at the far end of our yard, I pull myself up. I brush a bit of snow off my knees with my mittened hands and carry my illicit load toward the back door. Joey divulged the location of his secreted paraphernalia in our phone conversation just minutes ago. Great. But now it dawns on me that pipes and bongs and dregs of drugs are not easily disposed of.

What if, somehow, the stash is discovered between here and the dump? I don't want to be the target of a highly skilled SWAT team. So, I skulk around the kitchen. *What do I do? What do I do, what do I do?* Under pressure and with no other ideas, I wrap it all up in newspaper, run out to the driveway, and bash the parcel-of-trouble with a hammer. Shoving it to the bottom of the trash, I top it with scraps of the raw chicken I've been trimming for dinner. And some dog poop from the yard for good measure. I finish before Rick gets home from school.

Addiction doesn't start showing signs of trouble right away. Like cancer, addiction has stages. And, like cancer, it's not until the middle stages that symptoms of the disease become apparent. Joey is barely nineteen and his life is already out of control, so he has been an addict for a while. I'll never know when addiction first glommed onto my child; Joey probably doesn't even know. But, from the snippets he revealed during Havenwood's family program, I'm now aware that Joey played where addiction could catch him early on.

Joe and I, with our eyes wide open, had been asleep on the job.

Some things can be seen roaring in from a distance, like a tornado. Some things are just a suggestion in the shadows, like a monster under the bed. And some things are a mighty clobber out of nowhere—Chicken Little's sky falling down on unsuspecting heads. Well, Joey's addiction has been all of those things. At least to me.

Tucked in amongst the redbud trees and rolling hills of Kentucky, we raised our young sons in an idyllic place with charming old homes, front porches, stone walkways, and split-rail fences. A place where kids ride bikes and walk to school safely. It's where we lived from the time Joey was in the fourth grade to eighth. It's also where Joey, at some point, smoked his first cigarette, toked his first joint, and drank his first drink. Owl Creek is a small town; I knew all Joey's friends and his friends' parents. And we parents talked. But it seems he outsmarted Joe and me, though I don't know how. I was home when the boys arrived after school, and volunteered in the school during the day. I was around. I did all the things a parent is supposed to do to avoid the drug and drinking situation—or so I thought. When Joey was in fifth grade, he vowed never to smoke or drink or do drugs after participating in a class taught by local police. But, just as there comes a time when boys stop thinking girls are gross, there also comes a time when they reconsider their position on illegal activities.

Joey says it was in India, during his junior year of high school, that he really started partying hard.

"I was always overdoing it—drinking too much. Drugging too much. Throwing up out of car windows, or making a scene." That's what Joey said during family time at Havenwood. I'm shocked. Every time Joey returned from a night out, he reported to me for the Hug & Sniff Test before bed, and he passed inspection all but twice. I am reevaluating all the times I let him spend the night at a friend's. And all those empty liquor bottles discovered piled behind a little shed in our yard.

I had thought our cook in India was a tippler.

Was Joey's eating disorder ever an eating disorder? He admits now that he quit drinking and using drugs to please a girlfriend at that time. Maybe the eating disorder was a manifestation of addiction still in the early, stealthy stage. Maybe that's why he boiled over so quickly after leaving for college. If so, then Joey is quite adept at keeping hidden what he wants to keep hidden. It means he's been hiding addiction much longer than I'd imagined.

I trusted Joey. When he told me something, I believed him. For me to regard my child's every word and deed with suspicion would have been unnatural. It's been through trial and error that I've learned how to be a parent—but there's been a whole lot of error going on. Unfortunately for Joey, I guess I'm learning how to be the parent of an addict the same way.

Although I worry about Joey's future, I don't need to worry about his present. He's tied up in a safe harbor, so I'm enjoying some peace. And some peaceful thoughts. *Joey will finish rehab and devote his life to helping other addicts, while helping himself at the same time.*

Startled by the ringing of the phone, I hop up from my cottage cheese and carrots and daydreams. It's the addiction counselor at the halfway house in Minnesota telling me that Joey has been told to leave.

"Joey has been here for three months now, but hasn't been working the program. He's been lying about his job, working at a restaurant serving alcohol, not working retail at the mall." Words I don't want to hear. "He's been treating this as nothing more than a free place to sleep, wasting your money and a bed that could be used by somebody who really wants it." *Joey has put all his effort into wiggling around rules and wasting chances.* "Joey isn't taking his recovery seriously, and the strongest program, parents, or prayers can't do it for him."

Perched on the edge of the kitchen stool, I lean forward and slowly thump my forehead on the cool granite counter. *Why? Why? Why?* Joey is heading in the wrong direction; the relapse, not recovery, direction.

But am I surprised? About a month after Joey arrived at the halfway house, he called to say he had bought a used car—someone actually gave my darling little credit risk a loan—and was thinking of leaving, though was still undecided. He had completed a couple of the Twelve Steps, had a sponsor, and wondered if he was ready to try living the recovery life without everything being "forced." Thinking back, I remember that when Joey was at Havenwood, Joe and I told him we wouldn't pay for his flight home if he left treatment. I think when Joey purchased the car, it was the beginning of his plan to escape from up there and return to down here.

"Joey's addiction treatment hasn't been a waste," says Joey's counselor. "He will always carry around a knapsack full of tools he can use whenever he wants to. Joey has felt what it feels like to do the work, and he's seen what recovery looks like in action."

Joey is at this moment driving his "new" 1999 Dodge Stratus toward Bethesda. Barreling forward toward backward, his new-old car carrying him back to his new-old life. My mom has been busy praying for Joey all along, but I call to tell her to pray harder.

My pleasant daydreams of a few moments ago turn into gut-twisting what-ifs. *What if Joe and I hadn't moved so often? What if we had spent more Sundays at church? Or enrolled Joey in kindergarten a year later? Or bought less stuff? Or more stuff? Or doled out a spanking once in a while? Would the addiction bullet still have struck Joey smack between the eyes?* I know the what-ifs are a twisted little diversion keeping me from dealing with *what is*. But I entertain the what-ifs nonetheless.

What if, somehow, Joey had grown up in a world of just adults? What if he'd never felt the powerful pressure of prepubescent peers, or turned his back on the sweet inner self that caused neighbors and employers and tiny tots and moms everywhere to swoon? What if he'd never been exposed to the hollow world of our phony-yet-celebrated culture, with its shallow rules of engagement and endless enticement to fill up with easy, yet empty, pleasures? A culture sure to damage tender young souls meant for so much more? I believe that Joey started using substances to fill a chocolate-rabbit-like hollowness in his center, but this is not the reason he continues. He continues because, while filling his hollow center, he became an addict. These are two different things.

Substance abuse is the crack in the fragile façade of our empty culture. Addiction is the ruins.

Until Joey, my involvement with addiction was mostly peripheral. Oh, I was in the trenches a few times trying to help sort out some unsortable troubles, but I came and went, full of exasperation and harsh thoughts.

Mostly about willpower and sloths. Now I understand that addiction is a disease. Conquering addiction involves much more than the power of will. With a new set of eyes, I look at the people looking at Joey. Know-it-all people. Reproachful people. People in whom I recognize my former, unknowing self. Well, you can't know addiction till you live it. And then you still don't know it.

I long for the days when my dreams were our reality. Not sticky cobwebs on our nightmare.

Verse Six

MENTAL MOONSHINE

Mountains and molehills. Sometimes it's hard to tell which is which. Our house in Bethesda sits on a wooded acre atop a driveway long and steep. Once, after an ice storm, if it hadn't been for Shadow—our beefy black lab with toenails like cleats—towing me back up top by his leash, I would've been stuck at the bottom till spring. Tucked up and away from the neighbors and with Rick in high school (not play group) and Joey in trouble (not college), it's been hard to make friends since the move back to the US from India. Some days this feels like a mountain. But really it's just a molehill.

The days are heavier now than before Joey went to Havenwood, smothered under the weight of damned awareness. I can't hide anymore from what I know to be true; my son is self-destructing. I'm supposed to be the mortar keeping this family from falling apart—from tumbling brick by brick after the one that has already fallen—but *I* am falling apart. I wake each morning with only one goal: to put one foot in front of the other until I reach bedtime. Joe tricks his sadness into anger, but I cannot squeeze my naked despair into his emperor's clothing. Joey is dying a long, drawn-out death. And therefore, so am I.

In the three weeks since Joey traded hope for hell—since he left the halfway house in Minnesota and returned to Bethesda—I haven't seen him with my eyes, but scraps of recovery "his way" keep falling in my lap. Debt collector threats, car repo threats, probation officer threats. Everyone hunting down Joey calls me. I've come to hate our telephone. Hate it, hate it, hate it. Joe thinks it's possible Joey is fine, but I know Joey has relapsed. Like reading in Braille, I know what I know by the touch of my instincts. Joey's addiction came back when he did. It's sucking the life out of him in one long, deep, inhale. I know it.

Sometimes I think this is temporary, that Joey will get better and someday we'll have a normal life again. And sometimes, more frequently now, I think that he'll never get better, that this is our life forever. Well, "forever" meaning *as long as he lives.*

⁓

Clustered together near the front door, the ferns show off nicely. The last of them planted, I lean on my shovel and shake dirt from my hair. For days I've been digging ferns up from around our wooded yard, unsnuggling them from the ivy. They look better all bunched together up here. All week there's been a bunny nearby, munching on clover. So tiny and unobtrusive, its enduring presence is what finally catches my eye. I really see the bunny now for the first time and take a moment to smile at it and feel a twinge of joy. I allow myself to believe the bunny is a gift, just for me. An unabashedly fluffy and enticing gift, munching on lunch while waiting for me to open my eyes and heart to all the good things in my life. Of which there are many, but lately I haven't seen them. Whether it's a little miracle or just something I've conjured up in my head doesn't matter; it's still a gift. This little bunny has put a crack in the shell I've built around my misery. I hope Shadow doesn't eat it.

The Bunny Effect: One little thing can be a huge thing.

A little something that seems like nothing can change everything.

Joey arrives late and empty-handed, but at least he shows up; he's been avoiding us since leaving the halfway house and returning to Bethesda, so I wasn't sure he would come. Beneath the hand-hewn rafters and hanging baskets of a quaint little bistro, we celebrate Father's Day while at the same time playing the charade of a happy family. The making of a nice memory, even if forced and false, is on everyone's mind. Nobody asks Joey if he's drinking again. Or using cocaine and mushrooms and ecstasy and Percocet. Or freebasing and smoking pot. But he does need to know about the ceaseless phone calls from people trying to chase him down. He needs to know so he can stop the unraveling of his life, but he also needs to know that *we* know his life is unraveling. Again. Rick blanches as I thump the appetite-killing topic onto the table like a fatty slab of raw beef. This isn't what he planned on for lunch.

"I've taken care of everything, so anyone still calling is stupid," Joey says. And so the lies begin, spoiling my meal. Some stick in my craw, others stick to my brain where I'll pick them off later, ugly scabs to inspect at my leisure—and peril. Once we've pushed back our plates and loosened our belts, the waiter brings coffee and dessert menus, recommending the *tartouillat*, a cherry rum cake.

"You go ahead, but I won't eat anything containing alcohol," Joey says as he rises from the table. "Good-bye!" And he scuttles away. Back under the same drug-infested rock he crawled out from to go to rehab. The same drinking-on-the-job job. The same mushroom-loving girlfriend. My happy charade falls like crumbs from my napkin onto the restaurant floor.

Whenever Joey comes back into my life is when I feel his absence the most. His emptiness pours into mine, filling me with even more loneliness.

In gaining an addict, I've lost a son.

I've lost my son.

For a long time now, I've been careening through different stages of grief—cluelessness, denial, anger, and acceptance (ha!)—stuck for a while in one stage, zipping past another. An erratic pinball skittering around in a crazy, lonely place. Family and friends don't know what to do with me; nor do they know what to say. So they evade the messy, scary truth, resorting to platitudes that seem encouraging. But that hurt.

"This is just a phase. Don't worry."

"It's not as bad as you think; you're overreacting."

"Joey's young and crazy and sowing his oats. Everybody does it."

"I was wild, too, but look at me now; I turned out fine."

"It could be worse. At least Joey's alive. At least he doesn't have cancer."

Then there are the things nobody actually says but everybody is thinking. I know because I had the same thoughts myself before I knew better. And I can see it in their eyes.

"Rotten trees drop rotten apples."

"What a selfish, horrible son. My child would never do this."

"I would walk away and forget about the creep."

"I'm so glad we did everything right. This would never happen in our family."

"I guess the treatment program didn't work."

"Shouldn't you do something to help him?"

I understand the desire to spin my scoop of manure into something golden. But it leaves me empty, defeated, and very much alone. I'm worn out from trying to have my truth be heard, from climbing a mountain I shouldn't have had to climb.

My child is in the grips of a disease as tragic as any other life-threatening disease, even though it may look more like a disgrace.

If I say my son is an addict, believe me. Don't make me convince you. If Joey were dying a slow death from cancer, you'd accept the grim truth and reach out with comfort. I need that. Comfort. Joey isn't a bad person, and neither are Joe or I. You know that. Don't let the stigma of addiction stain your support as we do battle with this disease.

I'm tired of feeling alone. But still, some days I want to stay alone in my house on the hill forever. I want to avoid the bagel bin at the deli and the genteel corporate banquet—places where polite, safe banter is expected. Places where I chatter on about Rick—college tours, driving lessons, his job at the greenhouse—until it becomes awkward and I roll out the "Joey is taking time off from school" version of the truth. It's not that I'm ashamed, exactly, but there's a time and place for everything. Nobody wants to run into a big glob of unpleasantness while reaching for a pat of butter.

Joey? Well, he was treated for an eating disorder in high school; then, on his way to college, he got himself a Mohawk and was arrested for speeding and possession of paraphernalia. Two weeks later he tried to commit suicide, dropped out of college, became a raging drug addict, and had a few more scrapes with the law. He was in rehab for a while, but got kicked out and returned to his old life. So, he's probably not returning to college and probably isn't even going to live long. So . . . what's your son doing?

A few tenacious conversationalists have ended up with the whole sordid story in their lap. This is not a good way for me to make friends.

⸙

Pulling into the driveway, Rick and I see FIVE bunnies hopping around in the grass.

"Mom, you're surprised? They multiply like crazy! When you saw one you should've known you'd soon be seeing them everywhere," says Rick.

Okay, this is a sign. Since I allowed myself to see and appreciate one good thing, I will now see and appreciate more good things. My inner peace will grow and soon I'll be fat with bunnies. I'll be more full of bunnies—and inner peace—than misery. Misery, a burning-hot ember I haven't been able to let go of because *my misery is my son.* Wallowing vicariously in Joey's woes is a way for me to do something with my inability to do something; it's the only connection to him I have left. *Well, misery, begone. Make way for bunnies.*

An old friend reaches out across many years and miles with empathy and comforting words. She heard about Joey and knows firsthand how awful it is when addiction takes over a child.

"You can leave an addicted spouse if things get out of control, but you can never, ever leave your child."

She understands.

Five little minutes of commiseration, incalculable degrees of misery reduction.

The Bunny Effect in effect.

Having changed my clothes, I carry another heavy box up the stairs from the basement. I don't know what's in it. I don't look. I bump open the screen door and head to the garage, out of breath. Crippled by the layers of utter collapse and faltering transitions, until today I was unable to touch the boxes and piles left downstairs by Joey. Until today, dreams were in my way. Over the years, Joey dreamed of becoming a firefighter, a rodeo clown, a fisherman, and a marine biologist, but addict was never on his list. Nor was it on mine. My dreams never had me down one son and up one addict. I mourn the dreams that should have been, but today I'm moving those dreams to the garage. One small step in the misery-reducing direction.

⚉

I like it here. Nobody is bothered by my dirt cloud—the one that makes other people take a step back. At my twelve-step meeting for parents of addicts, I'm buoyed with hope—and pricked with envy—by the other parents' stories of strength and success. For those parents with stories less triumphant, I feel empathy. And a secret relief that our family isn't the only one still dangling over a cliff.

We are a hurting bunch, detaching with anger, detaching with despair, and detaching with denial, but we're all trying to get to the place of detaching with love.

For the past several months, while fumbling around with Joey's addiction, I've also been fumbling around with the addiction of an old childhood friend. *If Mary can get fixed, maybe there's hope for my son.* So I flew to Texas several times for the purpose of trying to get Mary in line. She told me she was in her late teens when she drank the drink that made her think, *This is IT,* and she has struggled with alcohol on and off, for many decades, ever since.

Force. Prod. Trick. I've gotten nowhere in my efforts with Joey or Mary. And getting nowhere has worn me down to a nub. Setting up the rows of hard plastic chairs for our meeting, some of the other early birds share their words of wisdom.

"The only thing you have control over is yourself. The only things you can change are your reactions and choices. Set boundaries. Build fences. Take care of yourself. Managing creditors or rationalizing with irrational drunks in the middle of the night hasn't changed or helped your addicts. But it has hurt you. Stop putting yourself in the middle of the insanity. Seek serenity in your struggle to Let Go with Love. And seek peace in your struggle to enjoy some happiness while the people you love are in such a bad place."

A middle-aged dad with old-aged eyes chuckles darkly over the gushing gratefulness he felt when his son was thirty-three days into recovery and hired for the nightshift at 7-Eleven. While this was the best news he'd had in a year, just a few years earlier it would have been the worst. The other parents buzz with their own reduced expectations and abandoned hopes. Bye-bye college and career and cute little house and cuddly little family. I listen, but I don't say that I have no expectations and only one hope left for Joey. I just hope he lives.

We're just a drop in the bucket, this roomful of moms and dads. There are millions of us outside these doors, but a deluge of raindrops doesn't make any single drop less wet. Our stories are similar—each one of us is hoping for a day more full of strength than tears—but it's in the details that hurt lies. Details we live with every minute of every day.

In 2012, more than 22 million people over the age of twelve were classified with substance dependence or abuse according to the National Survey on Drug Use and Health.[1] That is perilously close to one person in ten. Also, I've heard it said that for every person needing help with substance abuse, four more lives are affected (although this number seems low given all the lives Joey and his addiction have steamrolled). Altogether, that's almost five people in ten. *Almost half our population does battle with addiction in one way or another.* That's five people on a crowded elevator, or one whole side of the movie theater on Saturday night. Considering all the space addiction takes up in our world, there's a cataclysmic lack of understanding.

1   SAMHSA. 2012. *Results from the 2012 National Survey on Drug Use and Health: Summary of National Findings.* [Online]. Available from http://www.samhsa.gov/data/NSDUH/2012SummNatFindDetTables/NationalFindings/NSDUHresults2012.htm#ch7.3.1 (accessed 20 November 2013).

I came to the position of Mother of an Addict disastrously unprepared, but little by little I'm learning, becoming wiser, and getting armed.

⁀

"Hi, Joey. I'm just wondering how you're doing and what you're up to. Give me a call sometime. Love you!"

If I could string together all the phone messages I've left for Joey over the past two years, I would have a mile-long string of matching pearls—*Joey I love you, Joey I care.* As much as I wish Joey would call back one of these times, I dread getting a call that's *about* him. Tonight, and every night, as I lay me down to sleep, I lie down in fear. Someone told me that praying for strength doesn't mean strength will suddenly, magically happen. My spirit will not suddenly burst forth with the strength of spinach-fed muscles. Instead, God will give me a situation in which to find strength. Well, if I haven't found strength yet, then I don't want to. I'm not strong enough.

The stupid bunny packed up and left town, moving on to greener pastures. I haven't seen it—or its bunny buddies—around for a while. Nor have I been feeling any inner peace. That whole thing was just a batch of mental moonshine I brewed up, distilled from desperation.

Verse Seven

NOT MY SON

As with a secret garden, the beauty of motherhood is revealed only to those who walk its curving path. Only to those who answer to the name "Mom." Dry patches may seem to go on forever, and dust devils may be stirred up in passing storms, but there are unimaginable splendors that blossom out of nowhere, taking our breath away and keeping us Moms going. But, tucked away in the shadows, down a long bumpy road, there's a fetid place not meant to be entered—a place no parent should ever have to go. An unnatural place, where things meant to grow beautiful instead grow stunted and twisted, where arms are left achingly empty, and lullabies are choked out by lies. This is the place where love and addiction meet. The place where I live as Joey's Mom.

I lie in the dark without moving, ears perked, eyes opened wide. Someone is right outside the bedroom window, shuffling loose pebbles and crunching dry leaves and shaking what sounds like a spray can. I'm afraid the prowler might be Joey. I'm afraid he's drunk or high and spray-painting his hatred for me on the garage door in revenge for the words I said to him earlier this evening. Without waking Joe, I slip out of bed to peek through the blinds. Unable to see anything in the night but the night, I stand and look anyway, till the noises drift away on the heels of the feet that brought them. Holding my breath, I step outside. What I see in the moonlight is more sad than scary. A dozen balloons topped with a squirting of not-so-Silly String are rolling around near the back door. And a discombobulated birthday card with his own name, "Joey," instead of "Dad," written on the envelope is tucked into the screen.

"It's pretty sad your priorities are so messed up you couldn't even spare a few minutes for your dad on his birthday." I had called Joey soon after Joe went to bed. "Not even a phone call. You used to love making your dad's birthday special. Well, I have a pretty good idea what made you forget. And it makes me sick."

"Mom, why are you so mad?"

"I'm sad, Joey. I'm sad you've lost track of what's really important in life. And I'm sad you've sunk so low you don't even know you've sunk there."

At least I now know Joey can still be reached at some level—even if that level is shame.

⁓

I'm not proud of my Internet snooping. It would never pass muster with the folks at my parent support group, but I'm never going to tell them. A mother needs to do what a mother needs to do, and this mother needs to know what's going on. So, sitting at my desk, I troll through virtual (muddy) waters. I discover that Joey loves his *vida loca* and Ecstasy, but hates his job, Maryland, the thought of going to college, and his family. My online snooping drags me through mental spirals and loops, driving Joe and Rick a little mad. They saw Joey the other day and thought he looked good. Maybe even *all better*. They want some good news and a little optimism, but they will not get it from me. From their perspective, I'm a lead ball of negativity. Pulling. Us. Down.

Joey calls to meet up for lunch. Only half of me is ecstatic; the other half is suspicious, so maybe I *am* too negative. I brush my hair but don't bother with lipstick. It's funny how I long to lay eyes on the person who keeps flattening me. But my desperate wish is to say or do the right thing at the right time in a way that Joey might hear it. So I keep throwing myself in his path.

Pale and stubbly, the child who sits down in the wooden booth across from me does not look well. Joey's blue eyes are bloodshot and circled in shadows, and his hair is a dull, clumpy mop. Most disturbing, though, is the vacancy. Joey is not home. There's a wide swath of oozy scrapes down one arm—elbow to wrist and across his knuckles—as though he recently yanked it from a very tight, scrapey place. At my gasp, Joey slowly holds out his arm, slowly turning it this way and that.

"I don't know how this happened. Maybe I bumped into something at work."

Maybe, Joey, you're lying.

I notice a tiny red dot in the crook of his arm. Maybe it's an arm pimple. Or maybe he just donated blood. Or, maybe it's a needle mark and my son has been shooting heroin.

Without emotion, Joey tells me his car was repossessed; it disappeared one night while he was at work, but he now plans to buy a used truck. He rambles on, telling me the restaurant business is not a healthy environment to work in and that he wants to go to college in Savannah, Georgia, to be near his new girlfriend. I wonder how much she really knows about Joey. How much has he let her really see? It wasn't long ago that I thought a girl who dated Joey was the luckiest girl in the world. I don't think that anymore. I hate myself for having these thoughts. But there they are.

I call Joey's old halfway house, pleading for tips on how to fix the mess of a life he's making. I don't like what I hear, even though I knew I was going to hear it.

"Joey recently walked away from rehab. If he's enjoying this life he's chosen—not wanting or asking for help—then there's really nothing you can do for him right now. Something will need to shake him up."

I call Joey's friend (now roommate), Ivan. Joey rents a room in the basement apartment Ivan rents from the landlord upstairs. He called me when Joey went to Havenwood, so he must care.

"I'm not asking you to be Joey's babysitter, but would you please let me know if he ever needs help?"

"Sure," Ivan says. "But Joey is fine. He's even gonna take some classes at the community college. But I thought you knew that; he's always saying he just talked with you. This is really weird."

Yes, it is.

"And debts? Joey's always working so I don't know where his money's going. All he needs is some straight talk about what things'll be like if he doesn't get his shit together. I'll get the message through to him. He'll listen to me." Ivan goes on to prescribe family counseling. "You need to sit down together and talk things out with Joey. He's always felt cheated and slighted."

Cheated? Slighted? Joey shone like a star over our family and life. Both of our boys have been loved without reserve, and neither is second to anyone. This isn't a simple matter of misaligned perceptions—this is a matter of *maligned* perceptions. The addict is a liar. While the presence of a puppet master behind the scenes is clear to me, this unseen hand is not obvious to those who didn't know Joey before (or well). But I know the addict is deliberately misrepresenting Joey as a victim. What I don't know is how it's possible for Joey, who's known for his lies and bad behavior, to transpose badness where there is none *and be believed.*

I've done my share of enabling. Still do. Havenwood made that clear. Most of us enablers are well-intentioned; we act out of kindness, not realizing we've been led to the tip of the skewer by the addict. We try to rescue the addict from himself by fixing his circumstances and kicking his troubles down the road. Other enablers do the deed through denial, low stamina for high-alert, party-buddy preservation, or simply because they couldn't care less. And then there are the enablers who adhere to an Unwritten Code that commands loyal protection from "getting in trouble" for trouble that's already been gotten into. These enablers cover for even the most destructive behavior, like drinking while driving or overdosing. To be nice. To be helpful. *To protect.* A concept so simple, yet so misconstrued. When applied to an addict, the definition of *protect* needs to be turned inside-out.

Protect /prə-'tekt/: a. to make the addict violently angry and hate you and think you are mean; b. to reexamine the meaning of help and hurt, and to act on that new understanding; c. to be negatively judged by the whole world; d. to feel sick and tired; e. to suffer all the above for the short term for the sake of the addict's long-term well-being.

There's no telling when, or if, or how, an addict will hit "bottom," but "bottom" is not going to be hit while lying on a freshly made bed of roses. It'll happen while skating around on thin ice.

My son is a fugitive. There it is, posted on a website I check regularly (just in case). "Failure to Appear." A warrant has been issued for Joey's arrest for some unresolved crime and an ignored court date.

In the three months since Joey was kicked out of the halfway house, it seems he has been on a wild binge. A dangerous relapse. Not only has he been arrested, but on my desk sit several bills for Rescue Squad Life Support and emergency room services. Overdoses, I'm afraid. Apparently, Joey never officially changed his mailing address, and since he shares the same name with his dad, we continue to open unwelcome surprises. Joe and I sit on the living room sofa; we hold hands, recalling all the things we've done to help Joey. We need to remember this moment—the conviction of what we know to be true, right here, right now—because sometime down the road we will be mush.

My son is out of control, and he is going to die.

Distraught, I give Ivan, Joey's roommate, a call, fishing for information and hopefully a bit of truth. "*Warrant?* What warrant? No, Joey's got his head on straight," he says. "Joey's got a nice girlfriend, he hasn't been partying. Hospital bills? Don't worry. Joey told me he went to the hospital for stomachache." Hanging up, I hear an ambulance siren in the distance. It provokes a reflexive response in me, sort of like when I was a nursing mother and heard the cry of one of my babies, except this is neither natural nor nice.

A lawyer friend gives Joe and me a picture of reality: of an arrest warrant, of jail, of Joey getting raped—unwelcome images that hadn't wormed their way into my brain yet. He's shocked we aren't doing everything in our power to save Joey. *Snowball.* Suddenly Joey has a lawyer and Joe and I are left holding a solid ball of mixed messages.

What if Joey's newly hired lawyer puts a stop to the very thing that might, if left alone, put a stop to the rampage of Joey's addiction?

Joe and I loiter near the edge of the patio at the restaurant where Joey works, waiting to catch his eye. We need to tell him about the lawyer he doesn't know he has. As he turns away from a table of diners, Joey sees us in the shadows. His smile becomes a gash as he moves in our direction.

"What are you doing here? I'm not in the mood for your shit. The guy who lives upstairs with the landlord was found dead in the shower last night. Probably a heart attack. He was only nineteen. I watched them carry him out of the house. Whatever it is you're here to tell me, just fucking tell me now, and then go away."

"You didn't answer your phone so we just came by to tell you to meet us later, after work. We have important things to discuss with you."

"You know what? Fuck you. I'm not meeting you anywhere to talk about anything. Get out of my fucking life. I don't fucking want to talk to you or see you again. Not fucking ever."

I love the son that is mine—the son that's in there somewhere—but this is not my son. I don't know this person wearing my son's skin. This is a twisted caricature of Joey, and I hate him. My Joey is gone. Consumed by an addict.

I stand very still, staring at Joey. Waiting for him to calm down so I can help him. Joe, however, explodes. In more than twenty years I've rarely seen Joe lose his temper, but he loses it now. Leaning right up into Joey's face, Joe speaks in a guttural tone, using language apparently soaked up from his son.

"We fucking came here to fucking help our son so he doesn't have to go to fucking jail and get fucking raped. So if you want some fucking help, you fucking call me tomorrow."

I have no words. I simply follow Joe as he turns and walks away, and we drive home in silence. We should've left this alone. We should've let things unfold—or not—without getting involved. Whatever we do—however, whenever we try to steer things in a better direction—it just seems to make things worse. As soon as we walk into the house, Joe texts Joey.

```
I don't know what happened but it was bad. Let
me know if you want to meet with the lawyer.

Yes it was bad. Sorry, I don't know what
happened either. I do want to meet with the
lawyer, I have never *not* wanted to take care of
this, just let me know what I need to do.
```

I think we are all crazy.

When Joey climbs into the car, he looks and smells so bad, Joe asks how much he's been drinking.

"Some," Joey replies. "This better not take very long. What a fucking waste of time. I need to get to work soon. This fucking appointment is cutting into my hours." Joe pulls the car back over to the side of the road.

"This appointment isn't for me; it's for you. If you want to take care of the trouble you've gotten into, I'll drive you. But if you don't want to go, or don't plan on following through with whatever the lawyer tells you, get out of the car now." Joey stays. And stays quiet.

The lawyer is blunt. He tells Joey the warrant has been removed and he's got six weeks until his new court date.

"You'd better take the judge's orders seriously this time. If you ignore your original probation requirements or don't show up at court again, you won't escape the consequences; you'll find yourself thrown in jail. And if you can't post bail, you'll sit there for about a month waiting for your case to come up. Don't fool yourself; all of this will be on your record and it will really affect your life."

"And keep this in mind," adds Joe. "If you ever end up in jail, your mom and I will not bail you out."

College catalogues, guidebooks, and school rankings cover the old oak table. Shoulder to shoulder, Rick and I plow through the options, trying to chart his future.

"Hey, Mom, since I'm the first one going to college, the bar hasn't been set very high," Rick jokes.

"Rick, you are setting the bar now, and I'm sure you'll do it well." I feel my heart squeeze. Rick is now in the lead role, a role that by birthright should be Joey's. And, Rick has no older brother to look up to. His birthright.

I wanted my boys to dream big—not for their dreams to be controlled by poor choices. Whether Joey even dreams beyond the end of today anymore, I don't know, but his life is certainly controlled by his poor choices. I don't want Rick's life to go in the same direction. Now, as he's starting to apply to colleges, I worry. I wonder if Joe and I should try to protect Rick from himself by insisting he live in a drug-and-alcohol-free dorm. But I already know the answer. Rick must be allowed to make his own path. Any parental hurdles he finds in his way, he will jump. Just as I did. And Joe did. And Joey is doing now—but that's what is so scary.

I'm afraid for Rick, but I'm also afraid for Joe and me. I don't think we have the strength for another addicted child. There's no telling what may lurk in Rick's genes or if he'll engage in invincible thinking. Rick is strong-willed; he's never been easily swayed into doing something he doesn't want to do—often to my chagrin. But as much as I'd like it to be, this is no guarantee of anything. Joey is proof, as far as addiction is concerned, that good, strong character is irrelevant.

⁓

It's rare for Joey to drop in for a visit, maybe only a couple of times a year, but he wants to do so now, as Joe and I are on the way to a funeral in Kentucky. And Joey knew this.

"Oh, I forgot. Well, is Rick there? Can he let us in? Elise and I are in the mood for some hearth and home."

I don't know how to tell my son I don't trust him and don't want him in our house, so I don't.

"Sure, but no drinking."

As I talk with Joey on my cell phone, Joe calls Rick on his.

"Hurry, lock up the liquor. Hide all the house keys and car keys. Try to keep things under control."

The next day, Joe and I return home to the glint of a knife blade on the sidewalk and a hacked-up jack-o'-lantern bleeding seedy guts onto the grass. Our other pumpkins, those spared death by knife, have been chucked far out into the yard, mortally wounded. Cautiously, we look around to see what other damage Joey has done. The driveway is charred with the remains of a bonfire, the burnt bits and pieces within four feet of the house. And Joey's boxes, which had been neatly stacked on Joe's side of the garage (so I didn't have to look at them), are now tipping and toppling, belching bedsheets and pant legs. The hood of Joe's car is scratched from the drag of heavy boxes. Cigarette butts are burnt into the wooden planks of our deck, and the wrought-iron furniture is flung about and flipped. A plate of chocolate-chip cookies sits on the kitchen counter along with a cookie-baking mess and a note.

"Enjoy the cookies! I needed to get some stuff from the storage room but didn't take any liquor. I'm not as bad as you think I am. Love you!"

I'm sorry to think this, but Joey is nuts.

Rick says Joey seemed okay when he knocked on the door, but not wanting to have any part in whatever was going to happen next, he tried to disappear.

MY BROTHER AND I—A Conversation

Let me in!

Who is it?

Your brother.

Open the door.

Fine. What the hell do you want?

I just decided to stop by.

You're not supposed to be here. You know that.

So?

Get out of the way.

Mom and Dad are out.

Yeah, I know.

I know you know. That's the only reason you would be here.

Just stay out of the liquor closet.

Yeah, yeah.

I'm serious. If you mess anything up, anything at all, I'll throw you out.

Move your arm!

I'll be downstairs. If I hear anything, you're out.

All right!

You don't trust me?

No.

Not anymore.

You messed up bad.

Whatever.

Sitting on the couch, the sound of chaos rings through my ears.

This is a conversation I had with my brother, who is having problems with addiction. Though only slightly older than I am, he has been, for the most part, exiled from family matters. Despite this, I still feel the need to help him when I can; hence, in the conversation I let him use our house so that he can regroup, while still attempting to maintain control. This, however, is not what happens, and he ends up causing all sorts of destruction. Even though he may have "seemed" normal at the time of entry, I was fooled into his manipulation.

I found Rick's homework assignment lying on his desk.
Well.
Still waters have a lot to say.

⁓

Another emergency room bill. Another overdose. Joey is barely twenty years old and addiction goads him toward death: *Enough isn't enough— keep going until you drop. Swallow it. Smoke it. Snort it. Shoot it up. Be a statistic. Join your dead housemate.*

I feel the pounding of my heart. Pound. Pound. Pound. Like the pounding of nails into a six-foot coffin.

When it comes to saving her child's life, there's no feat too great or too small for a mother. Be it leaping in front of a bus or simply brushing locks of hair from a deathly white face, a mother is hardwired to act. But with addiction, a mother's helping hands are tied. All I can do with my helpless hands is write. I send Joey an email.

Dear Joey,

I miss you. My heart aches for you to be a part of my life. Will I ever again feel your hug? Hear you laugh? See you proud?

I stopped trying to contact you, not because I stopped caring, but because I had to stop the self-inflicted pain. I know what it means when you never call and don't come by. Your addiction, not you, is in control. You know the signs: the denial, the cover-ups, and the avoidance of friends and family; the legal and medical troubles; the unfulfilled goals. Your addiction is sucking the life out of you. It's sucking the *you* out of you. I don't want you to be an addict. I don't want you to push me away. I don't want you to die. I want you to be sober and happy and to fulfill your dreams and fill your soul. I want you to be *Joey.*

It's torture knowing that my adult son needs help and I'm unable to do anything but wait. Wait for that damn, scary, unknown, bottom. Wait for the death or destruction of the son I've loved and cared for since before he was even born. But how can I wait? How? How? How?

I'm terrified for you and the difficult life you are living. I'm sad for the life you could have. And I mourn the life I might never enjoy with you. You can stop this madness, Joey. I will help you to get treatment. I'll do whatever it takes to help get you on the right path. I'm here, just waiting for your word. I love you, Joey. I miss you. I miss *you.* Will I ever have my son back?

Love,
Mom

Mom,

I get stressed every time I see or talk to you. This is why. I'm actually kind of happy we don't talk anymore. I miss having a family too. At least you all have each other. I don't have anywhere to be happy for my birthday or Thanksgiving or Christmas cuz it sure as hell is not with you all. I have to rely on my roommates or work friends. Great huh? How can I be happy or feel supported when all I hear is you saying this?

Why would I surround myself with people who are more miserable than me? For once I am actually trying to move on in life. I would love help. Help that everyone my age gets when they go to school. Co-signers on student loans, the car I worked so hard for, a place to live so I don't have to work sixty hours a week. Go to school, get good grades, have a roof over my head. That's what I need right now. I already know you all don't care about that and the only help you think you can give me is rehab. Well absolutely not again.

So quit worrying and making your life miserable. Make the cut and finally sever the ties to me if that's what you have to do. Or let me live my life like I am and try to see what I'm doing through my eyes or any of the many others who see what I'm doing. Somehow even feeling this shitty and having had you ruin my night by sending such a lovely email I still do love you down in the bottom of my heart.

Joey

Verse Eight

HATE ME

There's not much distance between love and hate. It's just a few short steps between love and love-gone-wrong. But those steps cross a minefield. And addiction is there waiting. Because once love is eradicated—once addiction is in the company of only hatred (and fools)—it can, at long last, run amok.

Joey wants me to hate him. Anything nicer will just get in his way. The vile words from his email eat away at me—words that make clear what he's been trying for so long to say with his actions.

Hate me.

"So quit worrying and making your life miserable. Make the cut and finally sever the ties to me if that's what you have to do," Joey wrote.

Hate me. I'll make you hate me.

With the dexterity of the desperate, Joey has closed the doors on the people who love him. He's chased everyone away except those he needs: the weak, ignorant, indifferent, misguided, self-serving, or duped. The ones who will help his addiction. Not help him.

Well, Addiction. You can't get rid of me. I will never hate Joey. I will never stop caring. And I will never stop trying to trip you up. There will be times when I'm tired or stupid or tricked. And there will be times when I

75

don't like this son of mine. But don't be fooled. I'm full of love for him. It may not look the way love is supposed to, but my love is strong and it is forever. I will HATE YOU, but not Joey. So, Addiction. Go to hell.

❧

The expression "Letting Go" implies, well, letting go—as in dropping or throwing away—and as any mother knows, that's just not possible. There is no Letting Go in a mother's heart—not of a hand once held. Even if that little hand grows into a big hand attached to a horrid addict. But that's not what Letting Go means. I now understand. *It means to let go of the things that aren't mine to hold onto.* The things that have anything to do with addiction. The things that help the addict to consume my son.

In trying to cope with Joey's addiction, I've pored over dozens of books to help me Let Go with love. To help me survive. I carry one—all dog-eared, highlighted, and coffee-stained—everywhere I go. I feel stronger, more confident. Empowered. With my Paper Dragon breathing fire in my pocket, I'm ready to challenge Joey's addiction head-on. I will fight the urge to do things my way—so wrong, so many times—and I will seek a balance of wisdom and courage and faith (not hocus-pocus motions and wishes). I will be a formidable foe, a force for good, standing strong against Joey's addiction, standing strong for him.

Once upon a time there was a terrible flood, stranding a man on his roof. Falling to his knees, he prayed to God for help. As he was praying, a helicopter and boat passed by, but the man waved them away, saying he was waiting for God. The flood got worse and the man drowned. Arriving in heaven, he asked God why he hadn't helped him. God said, "I did. I sent you a helicopter and a boat."

I will be Joey's boat.

❧

Today, as though sour times haven't turned our sweet cider to vinegar, Joey calls to meet for coffee. He has learned how to maneuver with confidence through the wreckage he leaves strewn around, pretending—

to himself and to everyone else—to ignore it. Out of necessity, Joey is a nimble actor.

I dread the ugly scene sure to lie ahead. I'm ready to turn the car around when a realization hits me: I don't need to see Joey so badly that I must settle for his verbal abuse. *I feel the power of my Paper Dragon.* So, when I climb onto my stool by the coffeehouse window, I take a sip of hot coffee, and I breathe out fire.

"Joey, I'm happy to sit here and talk, but if you treat me with disrespect, I will leave. I'm done with your rudeness and meanness. So, if you want to spend time with me, make it nice."

Okay, it was just a dragon puff. But it's a start.

On the phone Joey had said he wanted to talk about his life, but now he says he wants to talk about his finances. Recalling the fleecing I took the last time we had this conversation, I mentally put my wallet in the vault and throw away the key.

"I want to move to Savannah, go to school, and get away from all the bad influences here. But I don't have enough money. If you and Dad won't help me out, I'll really have no choice but to live on the streets once I get down there."

"Joey, what you choose to do is up to you, but *I* choose to do nothing that might help your addiction—and I'm certainly not going to be swayed by what sounds like a threat. I would be a fool to give you any money knowing what I know about your life."

Many months ago, after receiving signals that Joey might return to college simply for the carefree, cost-free party opportunities, Joe and I decided Joey could invest in his education by taking out loans—loans that we would then pay off each semester in which he received decent grades. No skin off the nose of a student whose nose is deep in a book. Now Joey says he'll never be able to get a student loan with his bad credit. I think humans are hardwired to want to believe; mothers sure are. And I think addicts know that.

"Okay, Joey. Here's the deal. If you clear your debts and stay out of trouble over the summer—no arrests, no overdoses—I'll consider cosigning a student loan."

"Great. When I get the loan, I want control over it. I'll pay the tuition and stuff. I don't want the money going directly to the school."

And there it is. The whole reason for our meeting. Joey is after the money he could get from a college loan. A financial windfall to escape his ever-growing pile of problems here. A financial windfall to start new ones. He has no intention of actually going to school.

"Joey, drugs and drinking are a huge problem in your life. Not a solution. You can't run away from that. All of your troubles are a direct result of your addiction. Doesn't this scare you? Don't you want to quit using? Don't you want help?"

"Nope."

Joe is surprised when I tell him that Joey calmly sat through an hour-long discussion, especially one that was not exactly going his way. In retrospect—my view on everything these days, since nothing's ever what it seems at the time—I think Joey was high. He was unusually mellow and his eyes were red, so it probably wasn't my new ground rules that kept Joey in his seat the whole time. I wonder when I will stop being so naïve.

> Question about the A. Muscaria mushrooms for sale:
> I am doing research for a project on the toxicity and need
> to know if these are dried or fresh? *[Email from Joey to Electric Zebra Botanicals.]*

I find myself humming as I bounce around the house, smiling at the throw pillows I'm fluffing. Joey and I just had the most normal conversation we've had in years. I'm giddy—although I'm also aware normal shouldn't be so rare as to be so noteworthy. I called Joey after receiving his text saying he crushed his hand at work and was having trouble filling his prescriptions. He assured me he was okay and assured me he wouldn't take any narcotics for pain. Then we talked for an hour or more about the little stuff of life—what I made for dinner, the tribulations of clipping Shadow's toenails, and the color of the leaves still hanging onto the trees.

"This call means everything to me, Joey. I've missed you. You know I'm here for you, through thick and thin."

"I know. I love you, Mom!"

"I love you too, Joey!"

An image flashes in my head, unbidden, and my smile dies. Joey's face covered with blood. Fear? Omen? Either way, sheer horror.

"Bye, Rick!"

With Rick off to school, I pour a cup of coffee and sit at my desk. Almost the first thing I do this morning—and every morning—is troll through Joey's corner of cyberspace. It's also the last thing I do before going to bed. Every single night. And several times a day in between. Joe grumbles all the time about my obsession.

"Sandy, you've got to stop this. It isn't healthy; all this snooping around in Joey's craziness is making you crazy."

Joe won't step into the room, not one toe beyond the threshold. He wants no part in my spying activities. But when I look up, he's usually standing where I can still see him. He wants to know what I uncover. I may be the one doing the dirty work, but Joe needs this, too. This is our window into Joey's world and the truth of what's going on in it. Maybe it's a window that needs closing, but I'm not going to close it. Not ever. And Joe can't make me—even if he really wanted to.

During my usual morning rounds, I check the court website. Joey's been arrested—again. Drugs. Destruction of property. Theft. All this badness occurred on the same night I was smiling at throw pillows. Joe is out of town, so there are no eyes or ears around, which is probably a good thing. If eyes are the windows to the soul, then anyone could that my soul is bleeding.

Dozens of times, I dial Joey, but his phone goes unanswered. I get in the car and go looking for him, starting at work—except Joey no longer works there. He was recently fired for an altercation with the manager. I learn that Joey was habitually late for work, often not showing up at all, and the scuttlebutt is that Joey was taken to the emergency room twice within the past few days.

Hands shaking, I drive to where Joey lives. He must be so depressed and desperate with all the trouble he's in; I'm afraid he will try to hurt himself.

Locating the tiny brick house, I find a nearby parking space on the car-lined street. On the side of the house near the driveway, cement stairs lead down to what must be the basement apartment; I bang on the door, but there's no answer. I bang harder. Joey's glasses and a tube of toothpaste are lying on the sill of a knee-high window; anything beyond is blocked by a blue curtain.

Joey is sprawled out on the bathroom floor, overdosed, intentionally or otherwise. Dead.

I can feel it. I run to the door upstairs, the door of the landlord, and bang on it, too, harder and harder. But there's no answer there, either. I pace up and down the short driveway. What can I do? *What can I do?* I pick up a rock, testing its heft. But I can't break in. I have no basis for this or for calling the police. I need to get a grip. Joey is probably out with a friend getting loaded. Not lying on the basement floor stiff with rigor mortis.

Returning to my car, I sit and watch the house. I remember that a friend gave me the name of an interventionist not long ago. I look up the number and give John Southworth a call now.

"Do not hire an attorney to keep Joey out of jail. He's like a rabbit in a maze with nowhere to go. Joey needs the court to do its work. This is an opportunity for getting him into addiction treatment." I need to hear this because I want to help, not enable. "You could write an appeal to the judge requesting that Joey be ordered into treatment. But the most important thing is for Joey to stand in front of the judge and feel the fear. If Joey does end up in jail, I can do an intervention there. I've done it before. Jail, though it sounds horrible, is not the worst thing that could happen to Joey."

Looking at my watch, I see I've been sitting in the car, pacing the sidewalk, or banging on doors for hours. It's almost dusk, and there has been no activity. Joe's plane will soon land; I head home to give him the bad news when he arrives.

Joe's face collapses into a loose pile of wrinkles, like one of those shriveled-apple dolls. I wonder if the same thing is happening inside. Joe changes from his suit and tie and we drive back to Joey's house to pound on his door together. There's still no answer. On the way over I shared my feelings of doom with Joe, but he dismissed them. However, as I look at my husband who's aged twenty years in one hour, I know Joe senses doom, too.

A form appears under the glow of the streetlight: shortish, roundish, baldish. Keys in hand, he heads toward the front door—it must be the landlord. Joe and I step out of the shadows, a couple of overwrought apparitions gliding into his path. Nerves of steel, that one. He doesn't even react.

"Hi, we're Joey's parents. We're worried about Joey . . . we think he's on drugs . . . we need to find him." By some unspoken agreement, Joe and I don't mention his arrest; we don't want him to be evicted.

"Drugs? There's none of that going on here."

Oh really? That seems to be all that goes on here.

Joey calls, leaves a message. So now we know he's alive. The message plays, and I listen to the by-now familiar litany of injustices done to Joey.

"Hi, Mom. I'm on my way to see my lawyer. He's worth every penny since public defenders are all corrupt, conspiring with all the corrupt cops to get false convictions. I didn't call sooner because I was afraid you wouldn't believe me. But Mom, I'm innocent. This mess is not my fault; I still need your help getting the loan for college. Everyone I've talked to, even my lawyer, agrees with me; those cops were out to get me and owe me an apology. They even strip-searched me in jail, Mom. Down to my underwear. My rights have been violated. I hate Maryland. I just can't catch a break. Why does everyone keep picking on me?"

I have been beaten by cops for walking to take a cab rather than driving, and most recently was arrested for "breaking into a car" and "stealing CDs" within two minutes of leaving work. The whole system is fucked. It's all for show for the government to prove a point. Or for cops getting their arrests

for the night and making themselves look like they did some
work. None is true, legal, or fair but unfortunately the world
we live in is run by assholes who think that is right. So now we
all look at doing time. Glad we pay to be able to call 911 huh?
Those taxes get us soooo far. *[Social media post by Joey.]*

Gloomy days are unbearable. Smothering under sadness, I'm desperate
for big windows and lots of light. I hate clouds. Pressing down. I need to
claw for air, but there is no way out. There is no big happy family anymore.
Because one of us will always be missing.

We retreat each night to solitary spaces, worn out from a day of just
surviving. In the prolonged struggle of drowning, we've lost each other,
Joe, Rick, and I. Oh, we make friendly efforts, but *we are barely tethered
together.* We will never again simply be *a family.*

Clinging to what I hope is the sweet spot on the slippery distinction
between helping Joey and helping his addiction, I write to the judge
before the hearing.

Dear Judge Lee,

**I'm writing to you out of concern for my son. I'd like
to request that you consider court-ordered addiction
treatment as you review his case.**

**Joey isn't only an addict. He's a good and special young
man—a merit scholar and Eagle Scout—but mostly,
he's a loving son and tender soul who's become lost to
addiction. At twenty years old, Joey has already been
battling addiction for three or four years. He played the
lottery of youthful recklessness and he lost. This arrest
is an opportunity to get my son the help he needs.**

My husband and I are working with an interventionist who recommends at least one year of treatment, with the threat of jail time as a deterrent for noncompliance. As Joey's parents, our goal is for him to achieve freedom from addiction—not freedom from responsibility and consequences; as such, we have not hired his attorney and will not be part of any attempt to reduce his sentence.

I've come to believe that strong legal consequences may be exactly what Joey needs to shake off his addiction—but I also believe that a sentence to addiction treatment will be more beneficial than a sentence to jail. Time is what Joey needs. Time in the right place, under guidance of the right professionals. Time to stabilize his life and rediscover his old self. Time for lasting change. Time to heal.

If this disease continues to progress, Joey will likely be back in trouble with the law or he will die. I believe he needs to win the war against addiction in order to put an end to all of his other battles. Joey (or the addict within) says he will never return to addiction treatment again; it seems that an order from the court may be his only hope. It's terror for my son's life that has me leveraging this arrest to get him help before the inevitable, potentially fatal, fall. I'm pleading with you to force Joey to do time—a very long time—in rehab.

Thank you,
Sandra Swenson

I'm trying to shoo Joey to the small end of a funnel; I'm trying to make sure he has nowhere to go but rehab. Of course, that means I'm still trying to control Joey's life. But I'm still determined to do whatever I can to cram him into the place I think he belongs. Until I've tried everything possible, I won't give up.

✧

With every career move for Joe came new experiences and opportunities for our whole family. Joe and I grabbed Joey and Rick by the hands and whisked them through the wide-open window of travel and adventure. Together, we scuba dived with the manta rays in the Maldives and kayaked at sunset through sea caves off the coast of Phuket (Thailand). We tiptoed our way through spiny sea urchins and sand castles on the shores of the Mediterranean, sailed on a pirate ship through the Canary Islands, and explored the caves and volcanoes of Lanzarote. We searched for the Loch Ness Monster in Scotland, watched the changing of the guard in London, hugged a cork tree in Portugal, and hiked and climbed the Grand Canyon, Tetons, Big Horns, Austrian Alps, Yellowstone, and Great Wall of China.

These weren't just exceptional experiences—they were experiences exceptionally shared.

✧

Joey called Joe at work this morning to ask if they could meet for lunch. "Alone, Dad."

As in *Don't bring Mom.*

I don't know if Joe is nicer than I am, or if all the reading I've done on addiction makes me more of a threat—but I do know I'm definitely the parent Joey now wants to avoid. Joe's role over the past few years has evolved into something that looks like Peacekeeper. Mine looks more like Bulldog; I'm the parent more likely to stare Joey down. And growl. Joe and I have exchanged more than a few heated words over this, although most of the heated words have been mine. I think both our voices—joined together in one loud, clear battle cry—are needed to make Joey's addiction quake. This is a touchy subject.

Tonight, lingering at the dinner table after Rick leaves to do homework, Joe tells me about today's lunch date. Surprisingly, Joey didn't ask Joe to pay for his lawyer. He didn't even mention his lawyer or legal troubles through the entire meal. It was finally Joe who brought it up, and then Joey was flippant.

"It's no big deal; I'll get off."

Joe continues.

"Joey told me his new job doesn't start for a week and he doesn't have any money for food. He asked to borrow two hundred dollars to get by. I told him I loved him too much to give him cash he could use for drugs or alcohol. But I said he could always join the family for meals. I said he doesn't ever need to go hungry." I listen to Joe in silence.

"We were outside by this time. Joey started to beg, promising to pay back the thousands of dollars he owes us by the end of next week. I told him, 'Joey, it's not because of your debt that I'm saying no to you,' and turned to walk away. Then Joey said, 'Dad! Wait! What I really need is money for tonight. Elise is flying in from Savannah and I need to be there to pick her up. If you won't give me any money, would you at least drive me to the airport and take us out to dinner?'"

With tears in his eyes, Joe tells me he'd almost laughed at the time. Except he'd felt like crying.

"I felt like someone who barely escaped being raped."

Bewildered, Joe doesn't understand how he still, somehow, ended up giving Joey twenty dollars.

"My mouth was saying no, but my feet just couldn't walk away leaving my son empty-handed."

Joe says he feels like a two-hundred-pound weakling.

The real Joey would never pluck away at his dad's over-taut heartstrings. And the real Joey is not a sneaky, lying manipulator. Joey's light is still lit somewhere, but, as with a firefly in a tightly clenched fist, no one can see it. Not even himself.

GHOST OF JOEY YET-TO-COME

When Joey said he would come by for Thanksgiving dinner, or at least for dessert, I believed him. But his words mean nothing. Heaving a sigh, I bend down to pull the pumpkin pie from the oven. The too-long-in-the-oven crust has pulled away from the pie plate and the filling looks parched. The pecan pie doesn't look much better. I call Joe and Rick to "come and get it." I guess Joey can't be bothered to join us.

Rick comes into the kitchen. Laughing, he wraps his arms around my middle, lifts me on my tippy toes, and carries me around, demonstrating the way he lugs Christmas trees to people's cars at work. Such a small morsel, but it doesn't take much to feed a mother. *I almost feel happy. I almost feel like I matter.*

"The only one I'm hurting is myself." Addicts seem to believe this when they say it. But it's not true. I hurt in so many ways. I might still look the same on the outside, but every cell of me has changed. I'm altered. Hardened. Like a block of petrified wood. My thoughts are different, my beliefs are different, my notion of happiness is different. Joey's addiction has transformed me. I don't know if it's possible to go back to the blissfully ignorant but happy mother I once was.

⌘

When Joey walks through the door—a dark-hooded wraith out of nowhere—Joe and I are in the kitchen putting out ice and hors d'oeuvres for guests who will arrive any minute. Joey grabs a handful of nuts and pulls up a chair. He looks hung over, but I'm not going to say anything. This is one of Joey's rare appearances. I don't want to mess it up.

"Hey, guess what? I haven't used anything, not even a drink, for a few weeks now. Things are going really good. And I should be hearing any day now if I've been accepted into Georgia University."

Joey is lying. On all counts. But if I say I know he's lying, I have to say *how* I know he's lying. And I'm not going to do that. I've gotten very adept at finding things out on the Internet. I know Joey has not applied to Georgia University or any college. I know he's been partying and drinking and smoking pot. And I know he's filling prescriptions for Darvocet.

A codependent by proxy, Joe wants me to get the insurance company to somehow stop the filling of prescriptions, but I'm not going to do that, either. Joey will just find another source. *Or another drug.* I'm not going to do something simply to feel like I'm doing something. I'm too tired.

Joey says he wants to spend some long-overdue quality time with his brother.

"Hey, Rick, I have Ivan's car. Since Mom and Dad are having company, do you want to go for a burger?"

I can't bring myself to say I don't trust Joey; I just can't put that thought into words. So, as they walk out the door, I'm beating myself up. Either I'm a horrible mother for letting my addict son drive my other son anywhere, or I'm a horrible mother for even thinking one son might put the other in danger. No, wait. I'm both.

⌘

Swedish meatballs, buttered lefse, wild rice pilaf, and maple-mustard glazed carrots: our traditional Christmas Eve dinner. Festive aromas and carols fill our home, but Joey's place at the table stays empty. Pushing back our chairs, we move to the living room. Joe cranks up the volume and does an energetic jig to the tune of "Jolly Old Saint Nick" as I pass eggnog and chocolate snowflakes, always the boys' favorite cookies. When Joey and Rick were little, they liked rolling the little brown dough balls in powdered sugar and then watching through the oven window as they flattened and cracked as they baked.

It's not really Christmas Eve—we planned this little pre-Christmas celebration for Joey; he goes to court tomorrow and so might be sitting in jail or rehab on Christmas morning—but we play it through to the end. Sitting near our sparkly tree, Joe and Rick and I dump out the goodies from our stockings and we each open one gift, saving the rest for the real Christmas morning. I open my gift from Rick, a pretty pot full of paperwhite bulbs, soon to bloom.

Joey's gifts remain under the tree, unopened; his stocking hangs on the fireplace mantel all alone. I'm not surprised Joey didn't come, but I am surprised he didn't bother to call with a lie. Even if Joey had come, though, our evening would still have a hole in it. Because a hole can't be filled with something that's empty.

Not willing to leave Joey's court appearance in Joey's hands, Joe leaves work early to collect him. I drive separately, pulling over to the side of the road several times, feeling like I might throw up; the stress of waiting for the unknown is no match for finally facing it. When Joey arrives and sees me leaning on the wall outside the courtroom, he's not at all happy.

"You're here, too? No fucking way. I don't want both of you here. Go away."

"I love you, Joey, so I'm staying."

Moving into the courtroom, Joey huddles with his lawyer. Joe and I settle onto a long wooden bench nearby to wait for whatever's going to happen to start happening. We don't wait long. I should have realized his lawyer would get a copy of the letter I sent to Judge Lee. Joey turns on me in a screaming whisper.

"How dare you? I would have gotten off! It will be your fault if I get a fucking year in treatment. I will go to jail before I'll ever go back to rehab. Fuck you, I hate you. Get the fuck out of my life."

"I wrote that letter because I love you. Don't you understand that?" I whimper-whisper back.

Joey glares at me as he slides down to the far end of the bench. Turning my eyes toward the front of the courtroom, I see a case in progress. The defendant is asking the judge if he can pay his court fine later.

"Did you ask your dealer if you could pay him for your drugs later?" replies the judge.

When the bailiff calls Joey's name, Joey walks with his lawyer to stand before Judge Lee. The judge is wearing reading glasses and peers at a paper pulled from the file before him. Looking up, Judge Lee zeros right in on Joe and me. On *our* drawn faces, rather than any of the other drawn faces in the courtroom. My heart pounds. Judge Lee turns his attention to Joey.

"Are you under the influence right now?"

"No, sir," says Joey.

"I'm going to put you under oath and ask you the same question again. Do you know what it means to answer a question under oath?"

"Yes, sir."

"Now, I ask you again, under oath; are you under the influence right now?"

"No, sir."

"So, if I have you drug-tested today, it will be clean."

"Well, actually, no. I think the test would find there are still drugs in my system."

Judge Lee abruptly stops the proceedings, postponing the trial and sentencing until January. He wants Joey to be drug-tested daily, starting today. As Joe and I wait for Joey to sign some papers up front, another case is called. This guy might be sixty years old, but it's hard to say. Maybe he's only forty. A fumbling mumbler, he's gaunt and scabby, his hair too oily and sparse to look good worn so long. He looks like he might be smelly. And buggy. Judge Lee smiles at him.

"Harold, you have no idea how happy I am to see you here today." Turning to the bailiff, he asks for the courtroom to be cleared except for Joey and the other defendants sitting in the front row. As Joe and I get up to leave with everyone else, he tells us to stay. Once the courtroom is emptied, Judge Lee turns his attention to the twitchy man standing before him.

"Harold, could you please tell this young man about your history of drug abuse?"

And Harold gleefully obliges.

"Pot, cocaine, opium! I used *all* the drugs, man! Woo! Nine-teen-six-ty-fiiive." He's almost hollering, but his voice skips a note every few beats. "That's when the whole drug thing got started." His head jerks. He picks at his scalp. "I was just like you back then," he laughs. No. He cackles. And wipes spittle from his gnarly chin. I feel the color drain from my face as I watch this brain-fried and pitiful man. *This Ghost of Joey Yet-to-Come.* Looking to Joe for comfort, I see he has caved inward and is shaking. I touch his arm. He looks up, tears streaming. The meeting of our eyes puts too much sadness in one place; Joe stumbles out of the courtroom.

Harold continues, wild-eyed and rambling, his sentences going nowhere. And everywhere. He's homeless, can't keep a job, can't get along with people, and is in very poor health. And clearly he's lost a few brain cells over the years.

"So, Joey, where do you see yourself at this age?" asks Judge Lee. I can't hear Joey's answer.

Once Joe's emotions are shoved back down into the place they were yanked from, he returns to the courtroom and slips back into his seat. I reach out my hand. The bailiff leans over, asking us to follow him up to the bench. I've never talked to a judge. What are we supposed to do up there? Bow? Genuflect? Salute? Shoulder-to-shoulder, we move forward, the Tin Man and Dorothy, inching toward the great and powerful Oz. But Judge Lee is very nice.

"I know that was a very difficult scene to witness, but I wanted to make an impression on Joey. I have addicts in my own family, so I know about the lies, missed holidays, and moral collapse. I don't know yet whether jail or addiction treatment will be the best option for Joey, but how he behaves over the next two weeks will help me decide."

Winding through the corridors and into the parking lot, Joey won't look at or speak to me. He does, however, yell and cuss *about* me the whole way. Me and my motherly meddling. As I veer off toward my car, he won't even say goodbye. I hear Joe offer to drop Joey off for his first required drug test.

"There's no fucking way I'm going there now. Just take me the fuck to my house." And then, as I close my car door, I hear his seductive good cheer.

"Hey, maybe Elise and I will come over later tonight and watch a movie with you guys!"

I think my child is delusional. I think his brain is starting to melt.

> Hey everyone we need your help to free The King of Cannabis. Should he spend life in jail? Here is yet again another instance of the US government ruining the world! Everyone needs to band together to save this man. Pot hurts no one and I would gladly spend three years in jail (threatened sentence by Judge Lee in order to buy a vote from my rich and successful father for having less than a gram of pot) with this man to help save the rest of the world. *[Social media post by Joey.]*

For the people who know him, Joey's troubles are bewildering. Thief, vandal, addict. These words aren't compatible with grandson, friend, nephew, student, boyfriend, or kid down the block.

"Joey couldn't have done that; don't you think the police arrested him by mistake?" "He'll be where he belongs: in jail with all the other bad people."

Joey is a good person doing bad things. He has a really bad disease. Please don't forget the Joey from before. Please. Never forget.

To me, interventionist John Southworth is an angel. His business is located in Idaho, so we only talk on the phone, but he's always there when I need him. John was an addict for twenty-five years, in and out of prison and all sorts of trouble. But now he helps people like me and like Joey. A strong presence with a booming voice, he has guided me through many dark days.

And John does such a good job of intervening between me and myself.

"You absolutely must go on your Christmas ski trip. You need to live life. Your family exists beyond Joey. There's nothing you can do except sit around being miserable while Joey sits around being miserable, wherever the judge sends him. Your family doesn't need that. Go. Enjoy your holiday."

Joe and I had resolved to go ahead with our vacation plans as directed, but since Joey didn't end up going to jail, we didn't have to put our resolve to the test. Right now, however, my resolve is to not kill him.

Joey and Elise are skiing with us in Utah, and I can't wait to go home. This vacation is not a vacation for me. I don't know if Joey is high, is fighting the urge to get high, or has ruined his brain by spending too much time high, but I do know my sweet son is a lunatic stranger. Today Joey patiently adjusted everyone's skis and boots. Then he maniacally burned a tag off Elise's nylon jacket with a lighter (while she was still in it). He jumped out of our slowly moving car for no apparent reason—while laughing and refusing to get back in—and then gently guided me by the elbow so I didn't slip on the ice before storming off in a cussing huff about who knows what. My head is spinning.

Lighting the Christmas tree, I move to turn on the fireplace so Elise and I can defrost our toes. We sip hot chocolate and chat while the men get their showers.

"You know, Joey has woken up every morning we've been here with a stomachache and nausea. This happens a lot," says Elise.

"Well, I suppose that has something to do with his drug and alcohol abuse," I say.

"No, I gave Joey an ultimatum a while ago. He had to choose between me and alcohol, and fortunately he chose me."

I don't know enough about anything to say anything, so I don't.

Once everyone is showered and the spaghetti is cooked, we all sit around the knotty pine table for dinner. Passing the salad and rolls, Rick tells Joey he's been accepted into American University next year. I look from one son to the other.

How does Joey feel knowing Rick will be a freshman in college when he would have been a senior? If he hadn't been busy getting nowhere. Except into trouble.

"Hey, Rick, that's great! But I just found out I didn't get into Georgia University."

Ah-ha! The lie I've been waiting for. Thanks to my stealth operations, I knew this moment would come eventually. And I am prepared. *If I lie, I can force Joey to confess his lie.*

"Oh, Joey, that's too bad," I say. "But you're in luck! Dad knows someone on the board at Georgia University who can surely get your rejected early decision application moved into the regular decision application pile for reconsideration." I lie, lie, lie.

"Dad, can I give you my application to give directly to him, instead?"

I jump in before Joe can answer.

"No, your dad's friend can get it from wherever it already is." *Thin air.*

Hmmm. No confession; not even a speck of sweat on Joey's brow. And by the looks of things, I don't think Elise knows he's lying. So, what is the point of this charade?

Once we're alone, Joe tells me to stop rocking the boat. But I'm going to rock it. I just need to figure out when and how, and then I'm going to rock it even harder.

I guess these white knuckles of mine mean I'm not doing a very good job of Letting Go.

The paperwhites Rick gave me for Christmas bloomed while we were away. I bask in their beauty as I walk into the house—such a lovely greeting after a not-so-lovely week. The prolonged exposure to the wasting of my child's life and mind chilled me. Worse, Joey has no idea his mind is misfiring.

On the plane from Salt Lake City to Washington, DC, Joe mentioned that he told Joey that I wrote the letter to Judge Lee to keep him out of jail. But that's not true. *I wrote it to get Joey the help he needs—whatever that may look like.* Even if it looks like jail. Joe knows that. And he backs

that. He just didn't want to say that to Joey. Well, love doesn't always
get to wear a smile and be nice. Joe's not the only one who doesn't like
confrontation. I hate getting up in Joey's face. I hate the feel of tough love.
But if nose-to-nose combat might push Joey to face reality, then I'm going
nose-to-nose. It doesn't matter if I want peace or want to believe a lie or
want not to be spat on. It's not about what I want; it's about what's best
for Joey. There is no reward or pleasure at all in this; it's hard, it's lonely, it
makes Joey hate me, and I'm tired. I wish I weren't nose-to-nosing with
Joey all alone.

Verse Ten

THE STRAW

I duked it out with God last night. A middle-of-the-night confrontation that left me sprawled out on the cold, white tile of the bathroom floor.

While Joe found escape from our deteriorating world in the peace of deep slumber, I raged inside. Sleep wouldn't come. I stumbled from bed and down the hall, fleeing my tormented mind. I fell to my knees behind the bathroom door, buried my face in the crumpled folds of a towel, and pounded the floor. Because I couldn't reach God to pound on Him.

"Where are You? Why have You left my child? Why have You left me? I can't do this anymore. I can't do this alone. Why don't You answer my prayers? Why don't You hear me?"

Opening my eyes, I hoped to see God sitting at my side, listening. *Nothing.* He must have been busy elsewhere. Sapped, I curled into a ball, a limp lump between the tub and the sink.

"Please, God. Help Joey. Help him, please. Please, God. Please help my son. Please, God, please." Barking sobs faded into gulping whispers, which faded into whimpers, which faded into nothing. Faded until I had nothing left. Until I had given up.

Puffy-eyed and red-faced, I already know the day doesn't stand a chance. The raw wounds from last night bleed right into the fresh cuts of today. On the drive to pick up Joey for his appearance before Judge Lee, Joe and I brace for shifty and vile behavior—behavior we've come to expect from the shifty and vile addict living inside our son. Pulling my Paper Dragon from my handbag, I recite words of wisdom. Joe and I join hands. We take deep breaths.

Joey climbs into the backseat of our car and glares at me.

"Great. The whole fucking crew is rolling this morning."

And the day crumbles apart in large, devastating chunks.

"Oh, what's that in your hands, Mom? Your little self-help book for your fucking empty-nest issues? I'm done being your fucking project. Find something else to do."

I shrivel like a dying bug. The years and the fears devoted to Joey—the ones so twisted around my heart, my mind, my soul—suddenly constrict, clenching my entire being in a tight squeeze and strangling my words.

"Do not diminish my love and concern for you. You. Are. My. Son." And then I break. A gasping, heaving flood.

Joey pounds the back of my seat.

"Fuck this! I don't want to hear this! Dad, stop the car, stop it now. I'm taking a taxi!"

Joe says okay but somehow just keeps on driving. And somehow Joey stays put. And somehow, somehow, I keep on breathing.

"I hate you. I hate you both! All of my friends hate you. They all get help and support, like a car or money for college, things you could help me with to get ahead rather than always holding me back. You do nothing for me. You are the shittiest parents. I hate you!"

Joey sucks in some fuel to continue his torrent. And in that brief little instant, I decide to Never Accept an Addict's Lies as Truth. It's time to put an end to the College Application Lie. Right now.

"Joey, your dad's 'friend' at Georgia University says an application in your name doesn't exist. You never even applied, did you? It's all been one big lie. Were you pretending to have some respectable goals just to get your hands on some big money for drugs? Have you been lying to everybody? Or just us?"

Joey explodes, a crescendo of rage. Primal growl to quaking bellow. He twists and crushes a plastic bottle with his hands.

Joe shifts his gaze between the monster in his rearview mirror and me, the monster beside him.

"Maybe my friend can take another look. Maybe he just couldn't find your application."

Ignoring Joe's looks—the ones begging me to shut up—I plow ahead, between sniffles.

"Joey, your dad and I know you've been lying. About applying to school. About everything. And we know you're still drugging and drinking. You are lucky to have parents who love you as much as we do, parents still trying to get you help. And we'll still be here long after you burn everyone else out. Long after everyone else bails out on you. Take a good look at your life, Joey. Look at what you're doing with it. Who you've surrounded yourself with. And what real love means."

The wheels are still rolling as Joey jumps out of the car, spewing words dark and rank before fleeing up the steps of the courthouse.

"Fuck you. I don't need you. I've got really good friends who help me out in real ways and they always will. So get the hell out of my life."

Following well behind Joey, slowly, blindly making my way into the courthouse as Joe parks the car, I try to compose myself, but renegade squeaks and whimpers keep sneaking out. I push the heels of my hands against my eyes, trying to shove the tears back where they came from. When the courtroom doors swing open, I am coping. Barely.

Peering over his glasses, Judge Lee runs a long, slow look over the three of us. Then back to me.

"I've carefully read your most recent letter. It has been very helpful, but it must have been a very difficult letter for a mother to write."

Oh. I feel a tattered bit of hope. Maybe he has been moved to sentence Joey to treatment. Not jail.

"Joseph, your substance abuse assessment was alarming; you have a serious addiction problem," Judge Lee says. And then he gives everybody involved a chance to speak.

Stepping forward, Joey's lawyer does the job he's been hired for: speaking on Joey's behalf.

"It was only a small amount of marijuana in Joseph's possession. Also, my client cannot afford to pay for the kind of treatment his parents are recommending."

A lady with a flowered blouse and streaks of grey in her black hair stands up. It was her car that was bashed in. Her car from which the CDs were stolen. And her neighbor, my son, who did it.

"The aggression taken out on my car was so violent that he must have been on something more than marijuana." Turning around, she looks right at Joey. "He's a menace to himself and to society."

My son. A menace to society.

On the night of the crime, later on the same night his phone call had made me sing, responding police found the car with shattered windows, broken mirror, and banged-up body, a large rock lying near the front tire. The suspect—my little menace—was found nearby, crouching in front of a large van. He ran from the police, leaving the pile of stolen CDs on the asphalt. Frisked and handcuffed, Joey smelled strongly of alcohol and was carrying a cigarette pack full of marijuana.

I'm no longer coping. Joe elbows me. A box of tissues is passed hand-to-hand down the courtroom bench. Grabbing a handful, I press them to my face. Looking downward and inward, I try to rein in my emotions.

Judge Lee asks if either Joe or I would like to say something. I can only shake my head. I don't dare try to speak. But Joe steps forward.

"Sandy and I want Joey to get well. We believe addiction treatment is what he needs, and we are committed to paying for it."

Turning his attention to Joey, Judge Lee asks if he's depressed.

Standing, Joey says, "No, sir, but I'll see a psychiatrist if you would like."

"You've read the letters your mother wrote; you've heard your father. You know what your parents would like for you. What would you like to see as the outcome of this trial?"

Joey looks gaunt and shabby—his shirt is missing a button, the collar and cuffs are frayed and dingy, his suit is baggy and wrinkled. His "best foot forward" has taken a big step backward. But even so, Joey stands tall and somehow still handsome before Judge Lee and looks him directly in the eye.

"Well, sir, these past weeks have been really eye-opening for me. I now know I have an addiction problem and am ready to get sober. I want to have a life, fulfill my dreams, and go to college. But, sir, I know what I need to do; I don't need to go to rehab again. I can do it on my own by going to twelve-step meetings. I'm motivated this time."

Judge Lee takes another look at each one of us.

"I've made my decision."

I freeze. My tears freeze. Jail or addiction treatment? A bottom? A beginning? Or the beginning of the end?

"Since you have committed yourselves to getting Joey the help he needs, I'm going to commit myself to doing the same; but he will have to do the work," Judge Lee says, looking at Joe and me. Then he looks at Joey. "Instead of sending you to jail, closing out your case and moving on, I'm going to give you a list of requirements and postpone your sentencing. You have six months to prove to me that you're capable of getting recovery on your own."

Joey has six months to prove if he's the chaff or the wheat.

As he is led away to officially enroll in the county probation system, Joe and I push through the heavy double doors at the back of the courtroom and search for the quickest way out of the building.

Judge Lee cares. He is making an extraordinary effort on Joey's behalf. So, I want to believe it makes sense that Joey is walking free instead of being locked away somewhere, safe from himself. I want to believe God is working behind the scenes toward some rosy end I cannot see. I want to believe that fleets of helicopters and boats have been sent in Joey's direction, and that Judge Lee is the captain of the fleet. *But Joey had been right where we'd wanted him.*

He'd been channeled and cornered—poised to hit a bottom I wanted to have control of, a *not dead* bottom, dammit—but now he's back in free fall, with six months ahead in which to commit a worse crime, overdose, and die.

Joey finds every crack to fall or crawl through. Why can't he run smack into a brick wall once in a while?

On our search for the exit, Joe and I pass the little waiting room where Joey sits. We can see him through a glass panel on the door. He sees us, too, and waves for us to come in. Guided by indefatigable stupidity and hope, we do.

Joey stabs a finger at me, hissing.

"You and your fucking letter writing. It's your fault I didn't get off."

When Joe says he backs every word sent to the judge, Joey switches his one stabbing finger to two.

"Then it's both your faults. You just keep on fucking interfering. If not for you, the fucking judge wouldn't be trying to fucking help me. This would all be over, and I wouldn't have to do fucking probation and all this twelve-step and drug-testing shit."

"Joey, you're here because of your addiction and criminal behavior, not because of any letters," I say.

And then from his mouth, out rolls a dark stream of loathing.

"You are nothing to me. Nothing. Just a sperm donor and an egg donor. I wish I'd never been born. I hate your fucking guts and don't want to see you again. Ever."

The straw that breaks his mother's back.

The son I gave birth to has just hurt me one time too many.

One time too deeply.

"Joey, there comes a point when it hurts more to hang on than it hurts to let go. And I've just reached that point. I'm done. You can call me when you hit bottom, when all of your friends have abandoned you, and I will get you the help you need. But until then, I'm done."

Intent on cutting my ties—busily hacking away at the putrefied umbilical connection—I'm only faintly aware that Joey is talking.

"Good. You should have left me alone six months ago," he says.

And I completely ignore Joe. The peacemaker.

"You two shouldn't be saying things you'll regret later."

I've hit my bottom. I regret not my words, only that I've been driven to say them. I have given every ounce of me. I can give no more. I can do no more. I can take no more. And so, turning my back on my boy—the boy I may never again see alive—I walk out the door, letting it swing shut behind me.

Joe hangs back for a while, hoping, I think, that his proximity and patter will repair the day's damage. But when Joe catches up with me and tells me what happened, he looks the way I feel.

After I left, Joey had continued his rant. "Dad, if you would pay off my debts, I could get things right. But nooooo. Addiction treatment is the only help you're ever willing to give. You are so fucking useless. I'm so glad you are finally going to be out of my life. I hope you'll be miserable, worrying and crying about me every night."

When Joe had turned to leave, Joey said, "Dad, wait. I'll be only a little while. I need a ride home."

To which Joe replied, "You must be kidding."

On the drive home from the courthouse, I call Interventionist John. Feeling like The Worst Mother of the Year, I tell John I obliterated any good from the letter writing by giving up on Joey and walking out the door.

"This doesn't sound like giving up," he says. "It sounds to me like strength."

I don't feel strong. I feel like I swallowed a platter and it's wedged somewhere deep in my chest. I feel like I'm choking on something unmanageable while hoping not to die. I guess I'll know if I'm stronger than I think when I see what's left of me in five years.

I tell myself I don't care if Joey hates me; what matters most is that I try to do the right thing for him whether he likes it or not. But I desperately want my son's love. And I want him to know I've been trying to kick sand in the face of his addiction while at the same time trying to pull him to safety by the scruff of his neck. I don't want Joey to think my love and I haven't been always at his side.

As Joe and Rick and I sit down to dinner, Joey calls. But he doesn't call me.

"Dad, you have to let me move in with you or I'm going to be homeless."

Joe, still reeling from the day, somehow manages to deal with our little world-rocker perfectly.

"Well, Joey, your mom and I don't feel comfortable with you moving back here, not until you've demonstrated true recovery. But you don't have to be homeless. Here's the number of an interventionist we've been working with. He's a recovered addict now helping other addicts. He has been where you are. You can call John any time of the day or night and he will go to get you, wherever you are, and take you to help. Call *him,* Joey. Not me. I can no longer be involved in your drama."

"An interventionist? I don't need any more intervention shit! You should have quit fucking intervening a long time ago."

Joey probably doesn't even notice when Joe quietly hangs up.

Instead of putting my "Proud SDU Mom" mug into the dishwasher tonight, I drop it in the trash. It's too tainted with the dregs of hope for a certain stupid Egg Donor to ever drink from again.

I woke up this morning a woman spiritually shattered, but I go to bed tonight a mother thoroughly destroyed.

> I've been battling cocaine and alcohol addiction for several years. Recently I was arrested with less than a gram of pot. This is how I connect with my higher power, or a god, and am now banned from using my medicine, my connection with god through something he gave us to enjoy. My problem is I am on three years probation, drug testing twice a week, probation appointments once a week, writing in a journal that gets mailed to my judge once a month, going to an outpatient clinic, and seven twelve-step meetings a week. I am being punished for using my medicine for meditation and prayer. How is that right? What should I do? Even my lawyer is in awe by what the judge has done, and he's a very good lawyer. Help me? *[Email Joey sent to a marijuana advocate.]*

No one can ever tell me pot's not addictive.

❦

Over the past several weeks, Joey has called Joe a handful of times. When he does, it's mostly to talk about his twelve-step meetings, his great sponsor, and how much he's learning about recovery (ignoring Joe's updates on the ever-circling creditors). I think Joe is being charmed—the cobra to Joey's flute. But I'm not fooled. I haven't forgotten this has happened before, when Joey was at the halfway house. "Two weeks and a sponsor" won't lull me into being hopeful again. Nope. His words are just another blotchy mark on a history already stained. I feel bad Joe keeps on believing, and I feel bad I do not. I don't know which feels worse.

Several nights ago, surreptitiously observed from my electronic web, Joey made a frenzied, half-coherent attempt at actually submitting an online application to Georgia University (past deadline). Tonight he called asking Joe to look over his essay—and for Joe's credit card number to pay the application fee, to which Joe replied, "Nope."

My self-destruction began many years before I started college. I'm blessed to have a family that loves me and parents who've provided me with every possible opportunity and experience they could, but I was always struggling to feel comfortable in my own skin. I was shy and had a hard time making friends. I felt like the people surrounding me had everything in life under control and planned out, while I seemed to be missing the guidebook to life. This left me feeling scared and very alone. My feelings of isolation were strengthened by my family's seemingly endless pattern of moving from state to state or country to country every few years, packing up our lives to follow my father's work. It was the perfect excuse to never allow myself to open up. Instead I worked hard in school, studied SCUBA diving, and spent as much time on my own as possible.

In rehab many years later, I learned the empty feeling is called the "hole in the soul," and addicts try to fill this hole any way possible. My filler came in the form of a bottle of tequila. By the time I went to college, my condition worsened as my freedom had grown. I was filling the "hole" with as many things as I could, only to realize I was slowly killing myself.

```
I knew I needed help so I did the only
thing I could think of: I went home to
Mom and Dad. Less than a month later, I
checked myself into Havenwood Addiction
Treatment Center and discovered the Twelve
Steps of recovery. I found people like
me, those who had struggled as I had, yet
were laughing, smiling, and truly enjoying
life. They made me realize there was still
happiness to be found.

Today I find myself with true friends,
many of whom I met in twelve-step meetings,
and an improving relationship with my
family. Although my ordeal was incredibly
trying, I am grateful for everything I
have been through because it has made me
the person I am today. I finally have the
tools to fill the "hole" in my soul and to
be sober. I am a grateful Alcoholic.
```

I linger on the part where Joey writes that he has a family that loves him and parents who gave him every opportunity. It seems to be the only part of his college-essay-gone-nowhere that isn't a lie. (I continue to torture myself by reading everything Joey puts online. Every day brings at least one zinger.)

The revelation that Joey always felt shy and uncomfortable in his own skin comes as no surprise. But his *rationale* for drinking and drugging is *not* his reason for becoming an addict; those are two entirely different things. Joey tried to fill the hole in his soul with something that has left him with an even bigger hole, but *something else made him an addict*. He started out with one difficulty to deal with, but now he has two. Unless and until he addresses both issues—his personal turmoil and his disease of addiction—he won't be okay.

Dad, I'm really not able to work as much as
I need to. I'm barely scraping by as it is. I
honestly spend half of every day in twelve-
step meetings or traveling to twelve-step
meetings and because of that I miss out on so
many shifts. That's why I'm trying to get a
second job. Anyway, about all the creditors. I
have no extra money and can't pay; so now I'm
so worried about a warrant. Oh, and I would
really appreciate you not giving my new number
to anyone who calls. I cannot keep dealing
with the harassment. I'm doing the best I can.
I'm going to meet up with Elise in Savannah
next week and then we're going to drive down
to Florida for her spring break, just to
fish and hang out on the beach. I'm meeting
with my probation officer on Monday to get
permission. Love you. *[Text message from Joey.]*

My prayers aren't quite what they used to be. Now they come from more of a "what the hell, it can't hurt" position than a real belief that they will help. But when someone says they're praying for Joey, I'm grateful; prayers coming from someone with faith probably have a better chance of being answered than those coming from someone with an attitude and a grudge. Faithful people say things like "You don't know the big picture" and "With prayers it will all work out; Joey will find his way." *Hey, God, FYI: I don't want to be part of some "bigger picture." I just want our little picture, nothing fancy, and I just want it to be okay. Now.*

I've failed at every turn, even in my faith. But Joey needs *someone's* prayers. If Joey has to rely on only himself to get better, then Joey's in trouble. He's too sick to understand how sick he is—and the part of him that's sick is the part he needs to use to get himself well.

Tomorrow I head off on a much-needed getaway, a reunion with girlfriends from India. Joey's radar always seems to sense when my radar is out of range, though, so I fear trouble. Not one smidgen of me believes that Joey is okay. When Joey said to Judge Lee that he wanted to attempt recovery on his own rather than return to treatment, he meant he wanted to do things *his* way; he wanted to be on his own so he could continue to drink and use drugs. What he meant was that he wasn't ready to part ways with his best friends yet.

Of this I am certain.

I'm just as certain that it's only a matter of time until Joey goes under.

God help him. (I think I just prayed.)

I cannot.

PART TWO

The pause is as important as the note.

—TRUMAN FISHER

Verse Eleven

GREEN FROSTING
GIGGLES

I need to remember you, my son. The son before darkness.

I need to remember you, Joey.

Before I forget.

Before our story goes any further in the direction I'm afraid that it's headed.

I can feel you, the essence of you, the indelible imprint of you on my soul. But I need something more solid. Less wispy.

So I'm dusting off memories, the happy snapshots of you stored away in my mind. Everlasting pages of comfort for me to turn to, flip through, hold onto, when Lonesome for You gets too big. Like now.

But Joey, I've forgotten so much of what a mother should never forget.

Like threads of spun sugar, my memories of you are fragile. Burned by lies, seared by addiction, the tender remnants of *the you I was meant to know* are melting away.

The fluttery touch of your tiny hand on my arm, like butterfly wings, as I hold you close.

The waltz of our gaze, gliding beyond your blue eyes and through the gates of your wide-open tomorrow.

The sweet notes of your baby babble filling our home, like a song.

Your soft blue eyes.

Your nose, your toes, your belly-button, your laugh.

Your smile.

An orange-wedge smile. A green frosting smile.

A green frosting giggle.

A giggle during peek-a-boo, and noisy belly-kisses, and our first dunk in the pool.

"Mom, which 'guy' and book do you want me to put on your pillow tonight? I'll let you sleep with Teddy if you want. Dad, what about you? Or do you want it to be a surprise?"

A constant companion with a mini wheelbarrow, or a mini ironing board, or a mini shovel, grocery cart, or mower.

A gentle friend. A loyal friend.

"Hey, Mom! Hug . . . *toss!*"

Teddy's Best Friend and Caregiver, you'd plop the stuffed bear into a baby carrier for walks, or into Rick's high chair for a snack, putting Band-Aids on his boo-boos and teaching him about toilet paper.

Puppy forgiver. Even, eventually, when Shadow #1 chewed off Teddy's head.

A Bathtub Puppeteer: admission, one cookie.

A Snarling Tyrannosaurus Rex with dinosaur undies on your head.

An Adventuresome Pirate, sailing in your cardboard-box ship.

Favorite Color: Green.

Favorite Flavor: Green.

Favorite Books: The wilderness stories of Gary Paulsen.

Favorite Things in Life: Camping and fishing.

Your natural way of opening doors or carrying packages, and saying please and thank you with hardly ever having to be asked.

Reading. First me to you. Then you to me. Together.

Talking about everything.

Talking about nothing at all.

A tip-to-tip touch of your finger to mine. Our silent and secret "I love you."

I'm struggling, Joey. Struggling my way through a thicket of thorns. So many beautiful memories have gotten snagged on the ugliness of our now. And the thicket of thorns is getting thicker.

Fish. You loved everything fishy. Hooked from the first plastic goldfish you caught in the plastic pool at the fair. You named every fish in your fish tank and remembered them all in your prayers. You loved fly tying, fly fishing, deep sea fishing, shark fishing, teaching-your-brother-the-art-of fishing.

I remember the joy on your face as you rode your first horse and in your first jeep, bouncing across a rocky ravine or volcanic island with your brother. I remember the look in your eyes—and Grandma's—as you sat painting masterpieces together for hours. I remember the stretch of your hand to Grandpa's, heading off to feed the geese or build something out of wood or dig worms from the mulch pile. I remember the bit of bagel or banana you'd save from your snack for our daily walk to the pond.

You turned occasions into celebrations, and driving lessons into something less than awful. You fell asleep while showering for school in the mornings, hated being told you looked "spiffy," and went nowhere without music and headphones. You mowed lawns for the neighbors, cooked for your friends, made floor mats for orphanages, and gave a Delhi street dog and her pups a chance at life. You left people talking about you, the good kid.

A Son.

A Wonder.

A Shadow and Reflection.

A Giver.

A Brother.

A Buddy.

A Gentle Soul.

Slugged down and knocked out by the merciless fist of addiction. Even in my memories.

Like the first little curl I once snipped away from your forehead—*the last little tendril of yesterday is gone.*

There is no escaping the storm. There's only going through the motions while trying to find serenity within it. Says *me.*

Part Three

My baby grew up to be an addict. There was a time when I believed a mother's love could fix anything, but it can't fix this.

~SANDYSWENSON.COM

Verse Twelve

CRASH

Stepping out of the hospital for a few minutes, I gulp lungfuls of the moist Florida air. It's humid in Melbourne, even in the middle of the night. A bench on the sidewalk beckons. I shuffle over and collapse, wrapping my own arms around me, feeling lonely. It was such a pretty day earlier, a thousand miles and prayers ago, before the call about Joey—the call saying he'd just been scraped up from the wreckage of a drunken car accident and wasn't expected to live.

The normalcy of the day makes the unexpected even more horrifying. Leaning back on the metal slats of the bench, I knit together the hours— the carefree hours of my morning—with Joey's drive into oblivion. As Joey crashed, I was taking my first sip of hot coffee. As Joey's lifeless body tumbled onto the asphalt, I was sharing a good laugh with my friends. On the drive to the airport, unaware that my son's body was being rolled into the lonesome space behind an emergency room curtain, I was responding to my friends' concerned questions about Joey's addiction. As Joey's bloodied clothes were cut away by a medical team working to keep him alive, I was telling my friends that I don't talk much about Joey anymore.

"There's really nothing left to say. *Except to wonder if he's dead.*"

"But Sandy, surely he's just one of those kids who learn things the hard way."

"No, this is no longer about Joey making stupid choices. It's about stupid choices making Joey."

As Joey lay dying, I was strolling to my gate in the airport, heading home to Joe and Rick, refreshed after a wonderful weekend with friends. Until Joann, my sister-in-law, called.

"Joey was in a car accident. He's on life support, unconscious, and needs surgery. He was the driver. He was drunk. He wasn't wearing a seat belt." Joann's voice sounded oddly pitched and strangled. "Get here quickly, Sandy. Get here now." I knew what she was telling me; I knew what she wanted me to understand without having to put it into words.

"Stay with him, Joann. Tell Joey I love him and am on my way. He needs to hear that, Joann. I need him to hear that."

The police had tracked down Joann when they found Joey's cell phone. She was his most recent call to someone with the same last name. Of all the places Joey could have run amok, it happened within arm's reach of his favorite aunt. The police on the scene had thought Joey was dead, so a blood alcohol test wasn't done until he arrived at the emergency room. There, his blood alcohol measured a potentially lethal .35, yet he was somehow walking, talking, and driving. Until crashing.

Elbowing through lines of spring travelers, I rebooked my flight on a long and circuitous route from Kansas City to Florida. But at least I held a ticket. Neither Joe nor Rick answered my calls, so they didn't know Joey had been in an accident or that he might not be alive by the time I could get to him. I didn't want to know this all alone.

On the edge of midnight, my cab rolled to a stop at the front entrance of the hospital. Pulling my wheeled suitcase, I stumbled toward the place where machines and angels kept my son alive. The elevator door slid open at the intensive care unit. Joey's girlfriend, Elise, sat on the tile floor, knees pulled to her chest, arms holding herself together. A gargoyle. Shakily, she stood. Our paths had crossed only occasionally, but in that moment we were not strangers. I wrapped her in my substitute-mom arms. Suddenly Joann was there, doing the same for me.

When we were finally able to breathe, to talk, Joann and I foraged together for a grain of hope in this tragedy: Maybe this was the *not dead* bottom that we'd been praying for, the bottom that would lead Joey to want help. In a whispered huddle with Joey's nurse, hushed words were sent floating my way. Words I was supposed to catch without dropping any of them.

"Lucky he's still alive. Respiratory failure. Closed-head injury. Intra-abdominal hemorrhage. Copious secretions. Severely lacerated liver. Pain medication. Sedation."

More hushed words. "My son is an addict."

"Addict or not, drugs are needed so he will stay still, so he will heal, so he won't die," the nurse had said.

Now, standing up from the bench, I shake my head, trying to clear it. I need to get back inside, out of the darkness. I need to get back to Joey. Returning to his side, I hold the big hand that doesn't hold mine back and wonder if it belongs to my son or the addict. *The darkness has followed me.* From Joey's bedside I move down the hall. Elise and Joann sit in a small waiting room. I join them, closing the door behind me. Leaning forward, elbows on my knees, I sit on the edge of a green vinyl chair as Elise talks. More darkness.

"We've been here all week for my spring break; everything seemed fine until last night. He started drinking. We checked out of the hotel this morning, but before the drive back to Savannah, we went to the pier for one last bit of fishing. Almost right away Joey ran out of bait. He took my car to go get some more. And he never came back."

Elise had called Joey several times over the next hour, wondering what was taking him so long, and each time Joey had another excuse: a long line at the bait shop, heavy traffic, a mix-up with his order at Wendy's. During the last call, Joey's words had not been slurred, but neither had they made any sense.

"Elise, I'm here at the pier now, can't you see me?" Elise had turned to look for him, heard the blare of car horns, and the line went dead. Neither the horns nor Joey had been anywhere near the pier.

One of those honking horns had been under the pounding fist of Kim, a friend of Joann's. Driving down the coastal highway, she saw a speeding car shoot off the road and into a parked van, over several mailboxes and into a stone wall, and then bounce and spin back into oncoming traffic. Slamming on her brakes, Kim came to a stop just as the mangled car landed before her. Within minutes, emergency responders pried open the car door; as she watched, a bloodied head and arm lolled out; everything else of the victim remained pinned under the dashboard.

Extricated, placed on a body board, and intubated, there lay a handsome young man, unnaturally still, white, and dripping red. Thinking he was dead, Kim prayed for him—and for whoever would be missing him at the dinner table that night. Only later, sitting vigil with Joann when a nurse handed over Joey's snipped-off clothes, did Kim realize the young man she'd seen carried away on a stretcher was Joann's nephew. She recognized the pair of bloodied tan shorts.

Elise continues her story, belching up badness I not only hear, but can see. Joey shooting up speedballs—a deadly potion of heroin and cocaine. Joey overdosing again and again and again and again; another call to 911, another anticipated DOA. Joey, beaten up, punched, kicked. Joey, storing piles of marijuana in a warehouse for dealing. Joey, chasing Elise with the pumpkin-carving knife, and Elise trying to restrain him from jumping off our balcony. Joey, fired from his job last week for skimming money from the till.

"Joey says you and his dad never answered his calls. And he says he'll never go back to rehab because rehab doesn't work."

I don't want to listen anymore. I want to cover my ears. I want to hide. I want to sleep. The morning sun starts to filter in through the crooked blinds.

"I think you should let Joey return home after he gets out of the hospital. The reason he has all these problems is because you won't help him," says Elise.

One deep breath. Two deep breaths.

"Elise, Joey spent the last week with you on vacation, at the beach, fishing. He was surrounded by all of his favorite things, yet he still nearly drank himself to death. Joey is an addict. The desire and hard work to overcome his addiction must come from within; what comes from without can only support that. Support. Not do. Not cage. Joey had a network of people to reach out to, but instead, he cheated, misled, manipulated, and lied." I take a deep breath. Out comes a deep quivering sigh. "This is an awful thing for a mother to say about her own child, but it's the awful truth. Addiction is an awful disease." Elise looks like she may pass out from exhaustion, but I keep talking. She needs to hear the truth.

"Addiction pushes away the people who aren't helping it—the ones setting up roadblocks—but it clings to those who let it thrive."

Joann leans forward, putting her hand on Elise's arm, saying, "This is what Joey has been doing. He pushed away his whole family. All of us." Then she nods at me to continue.

"The truth is, Joey has surrounded himself with people who make his pathetic addicted existence comfortable. People who make it easier for him to use. Enablers. But where are the enablers now, this morning, Elise? Now that Joey is broken?"

The *other* enablers, I think, but don't say. Elise looks at her feet, but says nothing. I persist. "They're far away and thankful the damaged goods aren't theirs to worry about. If they bother to give him any thought at all. Enablers perform their 'good deeds,' do their damage, and then disappear when the going gets tough."

My throat is constricting. I pause before choking out my next words.

"No, the enablers won't lose a single night's sleep if Joey dies. But I will. So I will not enable my son."

Elise is staring at me with eyes too huge in a face too pale. Shattered from a day too horrible, she's unable to reply. But I don't care.

"If I were to take Joey home, Elise, would I lock him in his bedroom to keep him away from drugs? Would I slide his meals under his door? How long do you think it would take before I started to believe Joey's promises, which are always lies, and allowed him back out in the real world? Fewer responsibilities and no expenses is a horrible idea. I'm not going to set Joey up so he can overdose in a clean house with clean sheets."

"Or so he can kill himself or someone else while driving your car," says Joann.

"No, Elise, if Joey lives, he won't be returning home with me. I will not help to kill the son I'm trying to save. Hopefully Joey has hit bottom with this drunken car accident. Hopefully he'll really want to recover this time.

But he might not. If he doesn't, he'll be taking his stand. And I will take mine. This, Elise, is the very hard place where love and addiction meet."

This is the place where an unlucky son and his bitch of a mother meet, is what I read in Elise's sunken eyes.

Joey is not aware of his dad's arrival. He's not aware that his dad stands stooped and helpless by the side of his bed. I can do nothing but watch as Joe crumples at the sight of his battered son. I'm too crumpled myself. Joe looks at our boy. Our boy with such a long road ahead of him. This horrid, drunken, injured, sick, sweet-natured, remarkable, and precious boy who is our son. I see love and fear and anger on Joe's face. I feel it all, too.

Joey lies quietly now, but he's been swinging between unconsciousness and violence. One moment he's unresponsive to the sharp pokes of his doctor and the next he's yanking tubes from his stomach, lungs, and other mysterious places, lashing out at whoever's nearby. Apparently, Joey has a high tolerance for the drugs that are supposed to kill his pain and sedate him. Joey has a lung infection from aspirated vomit; his breath is so foul it's hard to get close, so I've mostly managed to avoid his fists.

Elise's parents have flown in to collect their stunned and stranded daughter. Off retracing yesterday's events, they will soon arrive at the hospital to meet Joe and me before leaving this hellhole for good. Tucked away in the lobby near a swath of potted palms, I'm half hoping they won't actually show up, or won't see us over here if they do. I don't know what to say or expect. *Hi, nice to meet you. We're Joey's parents. Yes, it was our son who abandoned your daughter, drank himself into oblivion, and totaled your car.*

Looking drained but determined, Elise and her parents trudge over to where Joe and I are hiding. From what they were able to piece together, it seems Joey went directly back to the hotel bar after deserting Elise, drinking heavily for about an hour until the bartender refused to serve him any more. Joey then got back in the car, driving north, away from the pier and Elise. In less than a mile he drove off the road going 55 mph. There were no skid marks; he didn't use his brakes to try to stop.

"Poor Joey. He's such a nice young man. He always seemed to be trying so hard, but could never get ahead. He had no car, no college education. It couldn't have been easy for him," says Elise's mom.

I open my mouth and out pours every detail of Joey's recent years. The whole ugly truth. I add that Joe and I love Joey and will never give up on him.

"But we have given up on helping the addict. We're done paying the addict's ransom."

Joe and I walk Elise and her family to their car. All four parents agree that this is a complicated tragedy and that both Joey and Elise need time and space to heal.

✺

Joe sleeps at the hospital in a chair next to Joey's bed. He began his vigil when the intensive care nurses needed help subduing Joey's periodic fights to escape during the night. Joey's quite strong for someone so weak; maybe he's detoxing—maybe somewhere in his unconsciousness he's running from big bugs or monsters. Joe continues to sleep at the hospital in case Joey wakes up during the night.

The hours and days have ticked by and Joey is not dead. In fact, he's begun to heal. Rapidly. So, Joe and I need to come up with a plan to keep Joey off the streets for a long time. A plan with some leverage. Because if Joey gets another chance at dying, he probably will. I imagine him walking out the hospital door and into a maniacal binge of whatever he can get his hands on. This cannot happen. Joey is sick and frail and damaged, and he must be protected.

I don't want my son to go to jail. But I also don't want my son the addict unleashed on the streets. And I don't know which I don't want more.

I should be weak with relief. Joey didn't kill anyone. He is alive, with no permanent brain damage, no broken neck, no broken limbs, and no missing limbs. His lungs and spleen will heal on their own, and with luck his liver will heal without surgery. Only a few stitches were needed, and all the cuts and scrapes will mend in due time. And, since Joey's blood alcohol level (BAL) was tested at the hospital rather than by the police, Joey won't be lugging a felony DUI around for the rest of his life. Everything, everything is fixable. If Joey wants to fix it—and *that* is why I don't feel relieved.

Interventionist John helped us to find a bed for Joey at a long-term addiction treatment facility in California, but we can't just scoop Joey up from here in Florida and deposit him over there. Not while he's on probation in Maryland. Besides, Joey would never willingly go. I try calling Judge Lee to tell him Joey broke probation by leaving the state and drinking and driving—all no-nos. I want to ask him to sentence Joey to rehab, even though I know he might instead sentence him to jail. But mere mortal moms cannot just dial up a judge for a little telephone chat. Nor can we leave a message with a return phone number, or send a fax. There's only one way to reach Judge Lee, and that's with a stamped envelope dropped in the mail. *But we're running out of time.* And we don't have anything to mail. To prove Joey broke his probation, we need proof he was drinking. But our adult son's blood alcohol results sit in his hospital record and out of our reach. His right to patient privacy comes first, even when protection of that right might risk his life.

While Joe and Joey doze on and off during the days—to rest up from their always-harrowing nights—I'm on the phone with police, lawyers, and social workers, and anyone else who might be able to show me some way to get Joey to the help he needs. But every which way runs straight into a brick wall. It's not easy to save a twenty-year-old drug addict from himself.

Theoretically, Joey can simply release his hospital records to his parents with a signature. Standing at his bedside, we present Joey with the official release form and a black ballpoint pen. Joey signs. Just like that. A hospital witness verifies the whole thing, and the proof we need of Joey's probation violation is almost in our hands. But not quite. The hospital doesn't give up copies of its records easily. Even with the signed document, there is fear of legal backlash; teams need to be assembled, meetings convened. Bureaucratic constipation. We can't wait around for things to get moving;

there are only three days separating Joey's confinement in the hospital from "Joey free to use." So, Joe and I do what we need to do to save our son. We steal.

There is a rectangular pouch on the wall outside Joey's door that holds his medical file. As nurses and doctors enter Joey's room, they pause to reach in and grab the bound-together stack. When they're done doing whatever they came by for, they put it back. So, it's right there, so easy for the taking, except that the nurses' station is within view. Neither Joe nor I has the guts needed for this. Joey is asleep as we hover near the foot of his bed, whispering about who should do the actual snatching. And then Joe suddenly does. He quickly shuffles through the pages and passes a short stack to me, then turns and heads down the hall in a casual stroll. I slide the stack up my shirt and stroll after him. Sweating, I keep my eyes straight ahead as we go down the elevator and walk through the lobby and out the front door.

And then we run. We run as though angry nurses are chasing us. *And maybe they are.* Jumping into the car, Joe races out of the parking lot and down the street as I crouch in the seat next to him, peeking over the headrest and out the back window. We aren't being followed, not that I can see. Once we finish up at the copy center, once the incriminating copies are tucked under the passenger-side floor mat and we're back on the road, we start to laugh and can't stop. Joe's laughter slows us down, but we're in a hurry. I laugh at him to go faster.

Laughter under control—once again feeling the weight of our crime— Joe and I stand outside Joey's hospital room preparing for the next phase of the operation. Joe walks down the hall to the nurses' station to ask a question, a little diversion while I slip the original documents back into the pouch. Then, giddy with relief, I smile down the hall at Joe, but he's not smiling back at me. Instead, his eyes are bugging out. I turn to see a short-haired blonde woman walking briskly in my direction. She steps right up to the pouch and removes the whole stack, saying she needs the records to make authorized copies for us as requested. My heart thuds. If Joe and I had laughed in the car for sixty seconds longer we would have gotten caught.

After sending Joey's legally obtained BAL to Judge Lee along with an explanatory letter by overnight mail, I finally reach Joey's probation officer.

"We want to keep Joey out of trouble until Judge Lee is able to order him to stay in rehab for a long, long time."

"I will get word to the judge, but don't worry. Since Joey's charges in Maryland are misdemeanors, he can go to the treatment facility in California and await Judge Lee's sentencing from there. But I never expected something like this from Joey. He didn't seem the type."

⁓

Joey starts to talk, but his voice is ruined from the tubes the nurse finally pulled out of his throat, so it's a struggle. He has no memory of the accident and is vague on events leading up to it. Of his time in the hospital, each day is a clean slate. Yesterday he remembered nothing before that; today he doesn't remember yesterday. But, no matter whether he remembers what he's saying or not, he is talking. Well, he's rasping.

Ever since leaving Havenwood, Joey has been drinking and doing drugs, even while he was at the halfway house. He had even planned to smoke pot, at least, as soon as he got out. When Elise started to harass Joey about his drinking, he started to hide it, drinking alone in his room; a fifth of cheap liquor at a time. He says it was better that way; he couldn't get into as much trouble as when he went out. Joey falsified his court-required attendance at twelve-step meetings, and stole money from the till and other employees' handbags at work. He doesn't know what made him drink on the day of the accident, but he says he was abstinent for about a week while on vacation with Elise. Stale crumbs of information— as always, too little, as always, too late.

Propped up in his bed with a pile of pillows, Joey watches a balloon bouquet float past the doorway and wonders why nobody sent him anything.

"I guess I don't have any friends."

I don't say that a drunken car accident isn't exactly a flower-sending occasion. Instead I say he'll always have us—his dad, Rick, and me—but there's probably not a lot of comfort in that. It certainly isn't comforting to me.

Joey feebly inches his legs over the side of his bed; he wants to go for a walk. He sits on the edge while I put socks on his feet. Leaning heavily on my shoulder, he shuffles down the hallway while I try to pinch shut the back of his checkered hospital gown.

Joey's first steps. We are almost to the nurses' station when a few notes of Brahms "Lullaby and Goodnight" drift down from above.

"Oh, Joey! Do you hear that? They play that whenever a baby is born—they probably played it twenty years ago at the moment you were born upstairs!"

Joey stops walking and, without a sound, he sobs. His head is thrown back, his mouth a silent gaping hole. He puts both arms around me.

"Mom, I've really messed up my life. I just want to be happy. I've lost everything good." Rasping, sobbing, not silently anymore.

Holding Joey tight, I take a moment to mend my heart. And I try to think of something comforting to say in response to what is uncomfortably true. With my fingers, I stroke his cheeks, wiping aside our mingled tears.

"Yes, Joey, you've really messed things up. But you can be happy again," I murmur in his ear, trying to soothe my broken boy. Leaning back, I take Joey's face in my hands, aiming his eyes toward mine, trying to reach him. Really reach him.

"Everything you've lost, including your happiness, is a direct result of addiction. But behind the addict is a wonderful person. I knew that from the first time I held you in my arms—just a few floors from here—and every day since. You are special, Joey. Do whatever it takes to find yourself again. Addiction is the only thing you have left to lose."

Weak, Joey gets back into his bed. He knows he will be discharged from the hospital any day now, but hasn't uttered one word asking about where he's going. Maybe he's afraid to hear the answer, but really, I think it's just that "something happening next" hasn't occurred to him yet. Joey's mind is not okay. I don't know if it's damage from his drug use or from the accident, permanent or temporary, but he's not himself. And this is scary.

"As horrible as it will be to look at this sick kid and tell him that going home is not an option, it's really the only thing you can do to help him." That's what Interventionist John said to me, and so Joe and I have pooled our determination so we can say this and mean it. We must. And we know it.

I fluff Joey's pillows. Joe adjusts the bed table and slides a strawberry smoothie within Joey's reach. We present Joey with his Three Options. Three grenades on a tray, from his perspective, one of which we've wrapped up in a bow: homelessness, jail, or addiction treatment on the warm and sunny beaches of Southern California. Stretching the truth on the DUI situation—since Joey has every reason to expect there *is* a DUI situation—Joe says we've cut a deal with the Florida police. He tells Joey that he will be allowed to do a minimum of one year in drug treatment in lieu of jail time, but if Joey walks, a warrant will be issued for his immediate arrest. Joey agrees to treatment, but only if it is in Savannah near his girlfriend.

"No, Joey. Your options are homelessness, jail, or treatment in California. Choose," I say.

He chooses treatment. Then, turning toward his nightstand, Joey won't say another word. When Joe reaches out to rub his arm, Joey roughly yanks it away.

The addict awakens.

❦

I prayed last night, thanking God for each and every miracle showered on Joey this week—and therefore on me—for once not asking for anything at all. For once, not feeling like I wasn't heard. But that was last night. Today, Easter Sunday, I'm basking in secret joy. Today I'm thankful because I get to head home to Rick, peace, and predictability, and Joe's the one responsible for getting Joey to rehab in California. Safely, sober, or at all.

Interventionist John warned us that Joey might become manipulative once he agreed to go to treatment.

"He might play the victim, trying to make you feel guilty and trying to negotiate deals. Do not buy into it. Do not give an inch. He's going into treatment because he got himself into this situation. He made his choice out of other choices. He might spout off some irrational goals or crazy ideas, testing you, trying to suck you into an argument. Do not engage."

What good advice. *A week of sobriety does not a recovery make.* The addict's talons are out before we even arrive at the airport. And it's painful.

But without John's guidance, the damage would be worse. After checking in, we part ways. My departure gate is in a different terminal. I hug my broken boy goodbye. He can't move quickly enough to escape me.

"Joey, one year will pass, whether you embrace recovery or you drift through it trying to fool everybody. Including yourself. My prayer for you is that one year from today, next Easter, you will be looking at a true new beginning and not at the same old messed-up life."

Please, not the same old messed-up life.

Verse Thirteen

SMUDGY WALL

Mothers in India often apply a dark lining of kohl around their children's eyes, a smudgy stroke meant to ward off the malevolent gaze of the "evil eye." A little flaw meant to draw evil away from perfection. Maybe this mother should have paid attention. Maybe, instead of flaunting with reckless gratitude a life full of good fortune, I should have humbly embraced a talisman of my own. From the loftiness of my lucky perch, I thought my perfect life was pretty nice, but also that perfect wasn't particularly interesting. Imagine. I cringe with shame at my arrogance. I should have been on my knees drawing a great big smudgy wall of protection around our family, because the glow from our spit-polished shine has attracted the eye of some vigilante equalizer intent on keeping us in its sights until we're completely destroyed. That's how it feels, anyway.

The wounds from Joey's car accident have not even healed—he's still hobbling around, careful not to jostle the liver that's still trying to stick itself back together—yet his fragile condition doesn't seem to be a powerful enough reminder of what brought him to where he is. Or where he could be. Like in a wheelchair, blowing little puffs of air into a tube when he wants to turn left. Or in a pine box, six feet under.

Joey plays rehab like a game. I had hoped Joey would be so humbled, so grateful, so afraid, so bottomed-out, he would dive into recovery with the same gusto with which I would throw myself into a fountain of youth. Instead, Joey moves the pieces of his enforced rehabilitation around like checkers, focusing on distractions rather than recovery, on regrouping rather than counting his blessings.

I *know* my son. I know how many days he could go before needing a really good washing behind the ears (one day) and how many hours he could sit, with a fishing pole in his hands, before needing food (six hours). I know the tone of voice he'd use when telling me he had done his homework but hadn't. And I know how nervous he was while learning to drive, even behind his Oakley shades and a swagger. I know my son, and he is not working on his recovery. It's the addict within, the interloper, who's at work, and who's working toward some other goal entirely. It's the addict who's cleverly maneuvering pawns around. It's the addict who plans to win at the game Joey will ultimately lose.

Joey calls from California daily, sometimes several times a day. I think he's unaccustomed to—and uncomfortable with—spending time alone with a brain that is drug-free. We've talked more in the past two weeks than in the past two years. But the voice in my ear does not belong to the child whose hand I held as he lay dying. This child is lying to me, manipulating me, tying me to him in an emotional knot. I feel the pulse of his every need, want, subtle maneuver, and calculated feint. I feel too much.

Joey breaks the rules at Sunrise Recovery, the house where he lives with other recovering addicts. Sneaking off to meet old friends, lying to the staff, playing staff against staff. He even lied, brought fetid wind to the old eating disorder, saying he was anorexic and wasn't able to afford enough food to keep himself healthy on the money allotted and so needed a larger allowance. His counselor, Gary, reported all of this bad behavior to me—which is quite the opposite of Joey's own reports of healthy progress—but this news is in line with what I found out during my cyber-stalking. I may not have the willpower to stop panning for cyber-nuggets, but I feel no triumph when I find one.

"If Joey keeps this up, my recommendation to Judge Lee will be that Joey go to jail," says Gary. "Rehab is not where Joey needs to be if he's working against his own recovery. I'm surprised Joey is twenty; I thought he was much older. It usually takes a good deal longer for someone to devastate a life so completely." Gary doesn't make me feel hopeful. "Joey's been manipulating his world around for so long that he's not going to unlearn that behavior anytime soon. Don't allow yourself to be manipulated. Not even once. If you show Joey even a hint of a crack, he'll be encouraged to chip away at you all the harder, which, of course, is really to chip away at himself."

"Not to worry. I love my son, but I've learned not to believe a thing he says."

Oh, I'm a horrible mother.

Something powerful has to happen to an addict, something that feels worse than either drugs or alcohol feel good. A bottom. Something like bouncing around the interior of a car like a lone sneaker in the dryer. But Joey was drunk or unconscious through all the dramatic, nightmarish stuff; in his mind it never happened. By the time he could make new memories, he'd been cleaned up, scooped up, and plunked down in a cozy cottage near the beach. So, though he might have bottomed out, Joey doesn't have any reruns to play in his head. He doesn't remember it. *Oh, Joey, if only you could take a walk in my shoes. If only you could take a walk on the path I've been walking as I've been walking after you.*

Rescued from himself, Joey also escaped taking responsibility for himself and facing reality. He blames the loss of his girlfriend, job, roommate, freedom, all of it, on being holed up at Sunrise Recovery in swanky Newton Beach, California. Blame is dumped like a heap of steaming manure on any doorstep but his own. Residents live in a new two-story home on a residential street just a block from the beach. A small houseful of young men cook and eat and sleep there, supervised by trained staff. Joey hates it. Hates it. Hates it. He hates everything about it. He also hates to hear me say it's not *where* he is, but *who* he is that matters (though I would think that living so close to the ocean would matter at least a little bit, in a good way). Sunrise Recovery was recommended as a place for addicts who've relapsed—a safe place for stepping back out into the world while learning how to live life without using. This had sounded ideal for Joey, but now I'm not so sure. My guess is that their program works best for people who want to be there—people who view it as a stairway to independence, not as an annoying obstacle.

Not once has Joey asked what or how his dad or brother are doing. Until I reminded him, I don't think he was aware that Rick is a senior in high school and will graduate in two months. Joey knows he doesn't need to work on our relationships; he can't even throw us away.

I don't feel any recovery vibes when Joey calls to say he is trying to complete the Twelve Steps of recovery in twelve days. Or when he says he's shocked by a fellow resident's relapse; to me this seems like he's shining a light on someone else's dirt so the dirt in his own corners will go unnoticed. And I don't feel any recovery vibes when I hear all of Joey's wants and wants and wants. He wants new contacts so he doesn't have to wear his glasses; he wants "his" car because taking the bus is inconvenient; he wants his cash card even though it's prohibited by the house rules; he wants Shadow, our dog, for company; and he wants a cell phone, with service.

"If you won't pay for this, I'll need to get a job and won't be able to focus on my recovery."

"*Really, Joey?* Are you listening to yourself? Instead of wasting everyone's time and money, why don't you just head on over to jail right now." I take a breath and try to take back my snippiness. "Joey, your dad and Rick and I are all making sacrifices. We've all had to give up things in order for you to be in rehab. You need to do the same."

"Oh, now you're just trying to make me feel guilty."

"No, Joey, I'm trying to make you feel reality. If you were in jail or homeless—which are your only other options right now—you wouldn't have a cell phone, new contacts, a car, or the dog. You wouldn't have anything at all." Joey is silent on the other end of the line.

"So, take what you have, your addiction program and your allowance, and make it work. Stop swapping your grocery money for cigarettes or cash. If you're going to put your life back together, you're going to need to live within your means, live the lifestyle of someone at your income level— an income level of zero. You are now officially poor, Joey, and you need to get that in your head." I hear rumblings of disgust emanating from Joey, but I ignore them. I'm on a roll.

"I'm sure that's hard to grasp, sitting there in the nice house by the beach, *but you are poor.* If you don't like your situation, then work to change it. All the energy you're spending on manipulating everyone to get what you want will keep you stuck in this cycle forever. Use this opportunity to your advantage, Joey." He starts to interrupt, but I cut him off. "Quit sabotaging your recovery. This year three people from Sunrise Recovery relapsed and died. *Three. Dead.* Don't be one of them."

Click. Joey hangs up on me.

Joey has no idea how hard it is for me to constantly wage war against an invisible enemy in what feels like a war against him. He has no idea the toll it takes, hating the addict and loving the son.

❧

Joe and I sit out on the deck to catch a bit of warm afternoon sun. I love it out here. The trees, the birds, the enormous pink blossoms hanging on the twining mandevilla vine Rick gave me for Mother's Day. Our house is the ugliest house on the block on the most beautiful piece of property in Bethesda. When we bought this place we planned to raze it within a few years and build our dream home. Several months ago the architect started to draw up plans. And so did I. Big windows to frame our small forest, his-and-hers studies, a huge master closet, a pool. Now we put the dream on hold; we don't know what will happen next with Joey. His first three months of treatment, just this time around, cost $30,000.

Sliding my chair a little closer to Joe's, I lower my voice and tell him about Joey's warehouse full of marijuana that Elise had mentioned at the hospital. This has haunted me. I had a dream the other night involving pot and police and prison. I worry about Joey being hauled away for the trafficking of marijuana just when he's got a chance at addiction recovery. Joe and I discuss ways to destroy the evidence—all of which involve skulking around a decrepit warehouse in the dark—and hauling, tossing, burying, or burning heaps of pot. We are demented. Really. At least we're sane enough to decide that our getting arrested would send a bad message to our kids. I call Joey and tell him to preemptively confess to the police. I'm quite sure this isn't what Letting Go looks like.

"Mom, there is no pot sitting in a warehouse somewhere. I made the whole story up."

So, is it a lie that his lie was a lie? Or is his latest truth true?

I try to find a way to keep Joey at Sunrise Recovery for an entire year and to postpone any jail sentence he might receive until afterward. I spend a good part of each day trying to sort this out: writing letters, making phone calls. I don't know why I behave as though I have control over anything. The pieces of Joey's life will land where they may, from where he's tossed them, up in the air—millions of feathers drifting and bobbing, caught on the wind, gently bumping into one another and off into another direction, impossible to control or predict, no way of knowing where to stand in order to catch a particular one in the palm of my hand.

Except they aren't really feathers; they're bowling balls.

And yet, I keep trying.

❧

Elise's mom calls. She wants help in disentangling my son from her daughter. A long-distance breakup has gone awry. I reiterate what I said when we met at the hospital in Florida.

"As worried as Elise is about hurting Joey, postponing the inevitable is just hurting them both. Joey's life is in his own hands; she can't save him or fix him or keep him from harm any more than she'd been able to prevent him from drinking and driving and destroying her car. But this drawn-out breakup is distracting Joey from fixing what's broken inside."

There are other things I want to say, but don't.

If Elise can't break this off cleanly and quickly, then she can have him. I'll put Joey on a plane and send him on down. But once she tires of daubing sweetness on the surface of his problems, she may not send him back. He'll be hers to keep. She just can't go messing around with something that's already a mess and then toss it back when the mess gets too messy.

Tell Elise not to help Joey waste his one last chance.

He's just one page in her life—just one quick flip—but to me he's the whole book.

I don't know when I last woke up happy. I don't know when the great hollow vacancy began to take up so much space in my emptiness. I don't know, because I've been busy just putting one foot in front of the other. But this morning the simple motion of lifting my head off the pillow is too much. Just. Too. Much. All because a rogue ray of sunshine slips through the window blinds and does the cha-cha on my face, taunting me, teasing me, with all its shiny brightness and the promise of a better day. *The liar.*

A little ray of sunshine. And suddenly life is impossible. Suddenly my whole family is washing down the drain unless I put the stopper back where it belongs. Because that stopper is the only thing between my grip on Joe's and Rick's ankles and our slide down into a deep, dark hole.

If not for Rick's still-occasional need for me to play a maternal role, I might not be able to do it. But he deserves more from me than I've been giving him, and so does Joe. Joey's addiction must not be allowed to chip away at Rick's last year at home or erode twenty-three years of marriage. Joey's addiction must not be allowed to destroy our whole family. The poison seeping into our household passes directly through me—sneaking in, I think, on the umbilical connection. Joey may be the one consuming the poison, but the poison is consuming me. The spread of this disease must stop. Right now. With me.

I will get out of bed. And tomorrow I won't get back into bed after Rick leaves for school. I will get myself dressed and brush my teeth. I can do this. I can go back to pretending that everything is normal. *Even as my child busily gnaws off his own foot.*

I will put on the dressings of normal life in the same way I shove myself into my jeans—take a deep breath, swallow the pain, and paste on a smile. I'll smile when I put dinner on the table. I'll even tuck a smile in my voice when I pass Joey's new address on to the next debt collector who calls. I will reemerge from the house, step back into the world I've been unable to face. A world where people do not, *cannot,* understand drunken car accidents or intravenous speedballs. A world snug and comfy in the illusion of sweet dreams, happy endings, and the power of a mother's love. A world that believes, because it must, that children do not self-destruct randomly and therefore this mother's love must be tremendously flawed.

But, on this, the world would be very wrong.

Judge Lee has ordered Joey to return to Maryland in two weeks for a hearing. I hope Joey will be allowed to return to Sunrise Recovery, but time in jail, with all its horrors, would be better for Joey than walking away free.

"I need to call my lawyer. I need someone to keep me out of jail. I don't want to be passed around like a bag of potato chips," Joey says when he calls.

"Joey, you never paid Mr. Parker for last time."

"He'd be an asshole not to continue representing me. And Judge Lee is an asshole for doing this to me."

It's interesting how people who have no respect for laws and rules and doing the right thing so often think it's others who are the assholes.

"You know, I wouldn't be in this mess if you and Dad had done an intervention a long time ago."

Joey is lucky he's all the way over in California, because if he were within reach I would slap my son for the first time ever.

Sunrise Recovery has been observing Joey for evidence of brain shear from his car accident. *Shaken brain.* They've been watching for abnormal behavior such as not remembering things or saying weird things. Joey does both. But it's hard to tell what might be brain injury and what might be mental illness, such as bipolar disorder or depression. Or what is Joey and what is the result of drugs. A lot of this stuff looks the same and overlaps, and it's hard to tell which came first. Joey never demonstrated any signs of mental illness (that I or his teachers could see) when he was little, but if anything was brewing as he grew older it got lost in the turbulence of adolescence or addiction. It will likely remain disguised until he stays in recovery long enough to see who and what is left once the party is over.

Sometimes I secretly hope Joey does have a mental illness. I would be released from the torture of wondering what I said or didn't say or did or didn't do to cause him to become an addict. I continue to look for evidence of my failure as Joey's mother even while holding onto what I already know: I didn't cause it, can't cure it, can't control it. *I can and will believe these things at the same time.*

When Joey was two, he and I would shuttle Joe to and from work on the days I kept our silver Buick Skyhawk for doing Mom stuff. Errands, zoo, play group, doctor. Around dinnertime, I would strap Joey into his car seat and we'd drive back to Joe's office. Sitting in rattan chairs with flamingo-print cushions, we would wait for Joe in the lobby. Even with my lap rapidly shrinking as his brother-to-be grew large, Joey always climbed on up to look at books or play with finger puppets. One time I'd forgotten to tuck a toy in my purse, so I rummaged around and pulled out a small pad of paper and a ballpoint pen instead. With his dimply little hand, Joey started to scribble. Then, peering closely at the pen, he dropped the notepad over the armrest. He unscrewed the pen into two parts. Put the two pieces back together. Took my hand and turned it palm up. He took the pen apart again, tongue poking from between his lips, but this time piece by piece until all the tiny pieces were in my hand. The silver clicky cap, the metal band, the coil. Then he put the pen back together. I watched. He put all the pieces back in the right places. I only held the pieces as he figured it out.

Like a peek through a keyhole, my online view of Joey's life is a tiny glimpse of what goes on behind the closed door; whatever lurks in the darkness around the edges is left to my imagination. But I don't have to work very hard to picture a day in the life of Joey. And it chills my blood.

While Joey is in rehab in California, I go alone to his Maryland apartment to move his things out. Down in the basement Joey called home, I'm once again collecting the things he left behind after yet another failed attempt at life. Joey lived in a dank, windowless room of this old house. A closet, really; a closet hovel filled mostly with a grimy mattress. The walls are water-stained and one is draped in plastic, partially obscuring a dark, gaping hole to somewhere darker. The room smells like something died here. Because something did. His pet rat is lying stiff and stinky at the bottom of its cage. I guess nobody fed it once Joey vanished. I don't even like rats, but I'm sad that it died starving and all alone. I'm sad Joey's mess of a life led to the neglect of things he cared about—even a stupid rat. I flip through a pile of bills, mostly unopened and mostly from collection agencies. Joey owes about $20,000 in debts, and someone is suing Joey for something.

I carry Joey's pitiful assortment of belongings upstairs in grocery bags. It's raining a little, so Ivan, Joey's no-longer roommate, stands with me under the raised back door of my 4Runner. Always a bearer of mixed messages, Ivan says he's surprised to learn that Joey never quit drinking, but then he also says he repeatedly confronted Joey when he rolled in drunk or high at five in the morning.

"I always expected a raid here. Joey wasn't exactly under the radar." Ivan had believed Joey when he said I was trying to get him locked up in jail. And he'd believed Joey when he said he didn't break into that lady's car. But when Joey said he hadn't stolen money from the restaurant where they both worked, Ivan knew he was lying.

"There was good reason that Joey got fired."

It's not all the little lies that have so much power; it's all the little beliefs. Every time someone accepts one of Joey's lies—every time someone believes the addict or gives attention to the actor—they validate, *feed,* the monster, the meter. They fan what needs snuffing. I wish Joey's friends wouldn't believe that their special word or deed or shoulder is just what Joey needs to get better. What he needs is professional help. I wish his friends would say, "Joey, I love you. I wish you well, so I'll be waiting for you with open arms on the other side of recovery," and walk away.

I wish his friends would remember that fanned flames burn quickly. When Joey's fire dies out and all that's left of him is ashes, they may shed some tears, but my life will never be the same. Not one minute of one day, not ever.

"When I was a teenager, I was an addict," says Ivan. "Then one day I woke up and decided to quit. And I did. Joey just needs to wake up, too. I know I've kicked Joey out, but maybe I'll let him move back in after rehab. Maybe I can help him."

Oh, Ivan, Ivan, Ivan. Have you forgotten that you still smoke pot and drink?

"Ivan. Joey will be an addict forever. He can never use anything—not pot, not alcohol, nothing—ever again. And until he gets a foundation of recovery under him, he can't even be around it. Perhaps not even then. He needs to start over if he's going to survive."

As in, stay away from my son, you pot-smoking boozer.

I don't know who drew the short stick in their relationship—the addict or the enabler—or who was more destructive to whom. Joey can learn to recognize and avoid the deadly pull of his personal relapse triggers, but there will always be people around to help him mess up his life. I know there's nothing I can do to stop them, but that doesn't stop me from trying. I feel like some fool at an arcade trying to slam down the heads of those little moles that keep popping up faster by the moment.

⌒⌒

So soon after the car-accident ordeal, it had felt like too much, too soon. I hadn't wanted to come here, but I did. I came because I needed to lay eyes on Joey. I came to California and Sunrise Recovery's family weekend with Joe for no other reason than that. Well, time is healing Joey on the outside, but what's going on inside still has a long way to go.

Joey will return to Maryland a few days after Joe and I go back home. Judge Lee has issued a bench warrant, so Joey will need to turn himself at the police station the night before his date with the court. Meaning a night spent in jail. But Joey doesn't seem to need any comfort; Joe and I are greeted with coffee and cigarette-fueled mini-hugs and then a view of his back. Joey is angry and hateful, sort of like a kid who's mad at his parents for sending him to his room for throwing a ball in the house and breaking a lamp. Sort of like a kid who's mad at his parents because he's being sent to rehab and jail for throwing down liquor and breaking probation. Desperate to make our tortured child happy and stop punishing us for something we didn't even do, Joe and I court Joey's affection. To win a glimpse of his smile, we grovel for things we can do for him and buy for him. Just as we did the times he was in treatment for the "eating disorder" and addiction before. Dysfunction déjà vu.

I hate that Joey hates me. I hope he won't always hate me. And I hate my hope that he will someday love me again.

But wait. Joey left a note for me on the seat of the car when we dropped him off at Sunrise following a tense lunch out. It's Mother's Day.

"Mom, I know I haven't been the easiest kid to raise, but you did everything right." I want to laugh. I want to cry. I'm not sure which to do first.

As I hang there—right there on the edge between teeter and totter—my cell phone rings. It's Elise's dad. He wants Joe and me to pay for a new car. His insurance didn't cover the loss of the one Joey demolished, and Joey didn't have auto insurance.

"You know what? Joey is an adult. He's twenty years old and hasn't lived at home for years. He is his own decision maker and life keeper. He's the one responsible for the car accident and the one responsible for making restitution. We had no more control over Joey getting into the car drunk than you had control over Elise letting him drive it. As parents, our responsibility lies in guiding Joey to recognize that he's an addict and needs help," I say, squeezing my phone in my fist.

"So I'm supposed to ask Joey to pay for this? How am I supposed to do that?" asks Elise's dad.

"Look, Joey is the responsible party, so he's the one you'll need to contact. I can't tell you how or when to do that, but I can tell you you're not the only one trying to collect money from him, so he won't be too shocked." Shifting the phone to my other hand, I continue.

"Joey is in recovery, he's working toward getting well, and even though he obviously has no money or income now, someday he will. The process of healing and following the Twelve Steps of recovery includes making amends, something that I'm sure Joey will strive for as long as he continues to work his program." I don't squirm through the long pause that follows. I. Am. Ice.

"What kind of person are you?" he finally blusters. "I would have had a check at your door right away, without even having to be asked. I'm out a lot of money; you're just going to leave me at a loss? I'm caught in the middle here. This isn't fair!"

"You're right. This isn't fair. Not for Joe and me either. Remember, there were only two people there on the day of the car accident: Elise and Joey."

"You're not being a good neighbor. You can easily afford this," he says, raising his voice. "You're just trying to make a point to your son!"

"You have no idea what I've been through, so don't assume you know what I'm doing or why I'm doing it."

Walk just one mile in my moccasins.

I dare you.

Joey has been in recovery now for forty-five days; he says he can't remember a time when he's been sober for even one.

Far short of the wished-for year of enforced drug treatment, life has caught up with him. He's coming face-to-face with hard consequences this time. Accompanied by a staff member from Sunrise Recovery, Joey has landed at Reagan airport in DC. The escort was a suggestion of Interventionist John's.

"It will keep you and Joe out of the equation; Joey will have nothing but himself standing between jail and the things he's done that landed him there."

No parental teardrops on the fingerprint pad.

Joey's been in jail before, but always while drunk or high. This time he's straight. And this time I'm also aware of what's happening. My son will sleep in jail tonight. At this very moment he's on his way to turn himself in and has called me before they take away his phone.

"Mom, are you there?"

An invisible something that feels like a lobster claw clutches my throat.

"I am, Joey. I just don't know what to say."

"It'll be okay, Mom. Thank you for not abandoning me."

A sob escapes me, because I can't remember the last time Joey said thank you for anything. I tell Joey I will be in the courtroom tomorrow. I tell him I love him. But I don't tell him to be careful during the scary night ahead. I just can't form those words.

Oh, how I wish I could be on my knees drawing a great big smudgy wall of protection around him.

Verse Fourteen

TWENTY-FIVE NIGHTS

Peering through the narrow windows of the double door, Joe and I hover at the threshold, unsure of what to do, unsure of courtroom protocol even after all the times we've been here before. Anxiously optimistic that Judge Lee will sentence Joey to addiction treatment—officially confining him to Sunrise Recovery long enough for things to sink in—we arrive early, only to face a closed door with a view of the judge already seated at his bench. Overhearing our whispered confusion, an officer steers us inside the courtroom.

"A prisoner was just escorted into the courtroom. Maybe it was your son; go on in."

Up front, wearing a baggy green jumpsuit, hands cuffed behind his back and an armed sheriff at each elbow, stands Joey. Expressionless, he listens as Judge Lee tells him he's a flight risk—as evidenced by his breaking probation and leaving the state. And, since his lawyer isn't present, Joey will be returned to jail, without bond, until some future, unspecified sentencing date can be scheduled.

Eyes sparking with panic, Joey looks in our direction. If comforting reassurance is what he hopes to see, he must be disappointed. I'm sure the only thing he sees is a reflection of his own bewilderment. Joe and

I move reflexively toward him, hoping, I suppose, to give him a hug—a "be strong" hug, a "we love you no matter what" hug—some kind of hug to make us all feel better. But one of Joey's guards steps forward, neck muscles bulging. One thick arm thrashes the air like a baton; the other is poised near his gun.

"Step back! Don't come any closer! You cannot come near the prisoner! Turn around and walk away!" The other guard whisks Joey out of the courtroom and back toward the cell he came from.

Reaching blindly for Joe's hand, I struggle to understand what just happened as he leads me from the courtroom. All the hope—the hope for something to finally save my son from himself—is expelled from my soul like the air from an overinflated balloon. I stand in the corridor. Just stand. Into my fog appears the face of Joey's lawyer, an apparition muttering about a mistaken court time and returning Joey to the courtroom. I turn to follow the voice, fumbling to gather up the hope skittering around like hundreds of marbles at my feet, but, as with all the other times I've scooped up my hope from where it has fallen, a few more stragglers get away.

Reconvened in the courtroom, Joey addresses Judge Lee.

"I broke probation because I'm an addict. I wasn't ready to do the right thing before, but now I've hit bottom. I'm a changed person since my near-death experience. I'm working the program, I'm staying sober, and I'm ready to comply with whatever you tell me to do this time, *but* what I'd really like is to return to Sunrise Recovery to continue my addiction treatment. I made a lot of progress there."

"Joey, I became personally involved in your case, but now have egg on my face. From your actions, I have no reason to believe you mean anything you say."

Turning to Joe and me, Judge Lee says he is going to postpone sentencing. He suggests we explore rehab facilities nearby. He's unable to maintain jurisdictional accountability over Joey in California, but will take our new findings into consideration as he weighs the rehab-versus-incarceration sentencing options. Until then, Joey will start clocking *time served*.

Joey is going to be locked up. For twenty-five long days. And nights.

Suddenly observing my world through an underwater spy-hole, I zoom in on Joey's trembling hands. His white face. His chin as it quivers. I wonder if Judge Lee is hardened to the crocodilian remorse of criminals who stand before him facing consequences. I also wonder what he thinks about the quivering chins of those criminals' mothers.

For the second time this morning, Joey shoots a panicked look toward Joe and me, but this time as the burly guards haul him away, I dare not move. He shuffles by, the clink of his handcuffs hanging heavily in his wake. The wake through which I now wade. Trying not to hear or think or feel.

A protective maternal instinct stirs inside me, but it's a warped mutation of the original imprinted code; there was no code created for a situation like this. I don't want this feeling, but it's the emotion that shakes out when a mother watches her child being dragged off to his cell. I force myself not to judge the judge; I need to remember he's not the bad guy. I need to look past the glint of Joey's handcuffs, past the desperation in his still-soft blue eyes, and back to what brought him in front of Judge Lee in the first place. I need to remember that Joey is being held accountable for his own actions, his own choices. Joey isn't the victim of anything or anyone other than himself today. Joey needs to see his world as it is—not through my pity-colored glasses—if he's going to work toward something better. But God help him. Nothing will be better if my young son emerges from jail more damaged than when he went in.

I need to keep moving. The crises, the traumas, the dramas keep coming, one after another after another, and I can't stop, can't stop or they will pile up behind me and I'll be knocked over flat. I need to keep moving. Then I'll be okay. I'm pretty sure of it.

Not much happens the way I think it should or hope it will—I don't even know why I think or hope it might. If I've learned anything hanging out in the halls of hell, it's to face the heat. Face the bad stuff head-on without wasting precious energy wishing for something different. Joey going to jail is not what I thought *should* happen, and it's not what I thought *would* happen, but it's what I've got.

Earlier, at the courthouse, the bailiff handed me Joey's personal effects since he wouldn't need them where he was going. Not at all bothered by ethics and boundaries, I go through the backpack and cell phone of my son, the inmate. Sitting on the floor of our living room, I page through a notebook, reading Joey's handwritten notes, and I scan through his text messages and listen to his voice mails. Joey may have remained sober while at Sunrise, but it seems to be the only part of recovery he was working on; the parts that might help *keep* him sober he was just working over. Using a familiar old sleight-of-hand trick, he'd waved his new sobriety around like a Tiffany's box, drawing attention away from the other hand busily restocking enablers, even while ridiculing recovery and the people and place taking care of him. Sneaking off, cheating the system, tricking, twisting, lying. Bending his recovery around any rules, and vice versa. Joey had put in time. Nothing more.

Some of Joey's bad behavior can be blamed on the ravages of addiction. The battle in the brain doesn't suddenly end with the corking of the bottle. But mostly, I think, the rake, the rogue, the lowest rung on the ladder, is the persona he hangs onto because it's who the addict needs him to be. It makes sense that the word *addicted* comes from the Latin word *addictus,* which means "slave."

I have put a lot of time into worrying about Joey and the continuity of his addiction treatment, and I was prepared to plead for his return to Sunrise. But now I see it's not continuity that Joey needs; what he needs is something to shake him up. I research tougher treatment facilities to present to Judge Lee. I hope jail time rocks Joey's world; I hope it rocks him so hard that he hits his seemingly bottomless rock bottom.

I want to push my son over the edge of the earth, and yet I love him more than the universe is big.

◦⟋⟍◦

Jail looks scary. The Maryland Correctional Facility is a hulking, concrete monolith with barbed things and razor wire. There are over one thousand inmates in there. I sit for a moment in the parking lot, car doors locked, and try not to be scared.

Buzzed in, registered, scrutinized, scanned, and thoroughly wanded, I make it through tight security, but my purse and the two little books of inspiration I brought for Joey aren't allowed in. I put them into a tiny locker. If I had been inclined to wear spandex or a miniskirt, *I* wouldn't have been allowed in either. Jail doesn't just look scary; it is scary.

Directed to a long, gray room divided lengthwise, I sit in front of a thick plate of smudged glass and wait for Joey to appear on the other side —the inmate's side. Looking around, I notice several cameras and a two-way mirror, and I have the creepy feeling of being watched. A few low-walled cubicles to my left, an elderly woman sits waiting, too. Somebody's grandma. She should be home baking blueberry pies or pruning roses, not waiting in this cement-block staging area for her beloved criminal to appear. Well, you just can't tell what burdens people carry around, not simply by looking. You never know what sadness lurks under the deceptively placid façade of bluish-white hair and support hose—or behind the smile of a certain forty-eight-year-old mother adept at concealing more than just sags and wrinkles.

A guard delivers Joey to the blue plastic chair across from me and quickly disappears. Joey hasn't shaven, his hair isn't combed, and he wears a rumpled jumpsuit, but he grins. He's happy I'm here. Well, he's happy to have a visitor. Before reaching for the grimy handsets, we look at each other for a moment and wipe away a few tears. I put my hand up to the glass between us and Joey puts his hand up to mine. Just like in the movies. Because we have nothing else to go on.

We put the handsets to our ears.

"Yes, Mom, I'm safe."

Joey spends twenty-three hours a day in the cell he shares with a drug dealer. He has one hour to shower, make phone calls, or watch TV. Time drags, he sleeps a lot, and he's always hungry. But nobody steals his food; I know because I ask. He's run into several people he knows in prison, but they are reminders of what he is missing and make him want to get out and use. Joey tells me that smoking pot leads him to drinking, which leads him to everything else. He now knows he can't ever smoke pot again, even though he wishes he could. There's not one shred of doubt left that Joey is an addict; he doesn't even bother to pretend otherwise anymore.

Joey shows me his standard-issue, unbreakable, weapon-proof pen. Then he laments the great injustice inflicted upon him. He wants me to hire someone from Sunrise Recovery to come educate Judge Lee about addiction being a disease. I remind Joey that he isn't in prison for being an addict—he's in prison for the crimes he committed while an addict.

"Joey, being the one does not excuse the other."

When Joe and I were at Sunrise's family program, we attended a lecture on addiction and crime given by a specialist in the field.

"Though the behavior of addicts often makes them look like sociopaths, addicts are not bad people. They are sick people," he said. "Addiction is an epidemic in the United States, and treatment for it should be covered by insurance, the same as any other disease. Most people locked up in jail are there for drug-related crimes, but addicts need to be in drug treatment, not jail. Diabetics aren't put in jail; they receive treatment for their disease, covered by insurance. Of course, addicts who commit a crime must pay the penalty. The key is that they need to get treatment *before* a crime is committed."

Well, it's nearly impossible to get an addict who's over eighteen into treatment if he doesn't want to go. And he probably won't want help until he is in some kind of trouble—something like committing a crime and going to jail.

The conundrums are endless. If an addict is put on probation for committing a crime, free to get help for addiction (not trapped behind bars), chances are he won't; an addict's whims are fickle. But if the addict *can* be convinced (or forced, or even just remember) to get help, insurance won't pay for inpatient treatment, not until the addict fails in a few outpatient programs first. Outpatient programs, however, leave addicts free to do drugs and drug-related crimes, and land in jail, and not get drug treatment. There's a colossal chasm between what should be and what is. And Joey is in it.

A short hour after my arrival, a guard taps Joey on the shoulder. Our time is up. I press my hand back up to the cold, impenetrable glass.

"Joey, never underestimate my love for you. No matter what you've done, no matter what you might do, I may not like it, but I will always love you."

I carry my cell phone and a hot cup of coffee outside onto the deck. Late morning here in Bethesda, it's barely dawn out west, but I can't wait any longer; I make my call to John Southworth. The Interventionist. The faceless man behind the warm, rumbly voice. The keel that has kept me from capsizing through so many storms. He's such an important person in my life, and doesn't even know it. When I hear the calm confidence in his words, I feel strength.

"Jail isn't the worst thing that can happen to Joey, and it's probably not nearly as bad as some of the things he lived through over the past several years. He needs this dose of reality. He needs to see that life has rules and there are consequences for breaking those rules—a lesson he's managed to artfully dodge up until now. Joey has what we call a low bottom. He hasn't gotten the meaning of recovery even though he's been in and out of treatment and all kinds of bad trouble. And he still might not be at his bottom; it might take ten years and a stint at the Salvation Army before he gets there. But there's nothing you can do to change his path."

John and I discuss various rehabs, eliminating Sunrise Recovery, and narrow down the remaining contenders for my recommendation to Judge Lee. I confess the latest worry keeping me awake at night.

"The Serenity Prayer says, 'God, grant me the serenity to accept the things I cannot change, the courage to change the things I can, and the wisdom to know the difference.' But how do I tell the difference between what I *can* change and what I *should* change?" I ask John, and then ramble on without waiting for his answer. "Whatever happens next is Joey's best chance to beat his addiction. So this is my best chance at making sure he gets it right. All these treatment facilities sound good, but what if I pick one that is wrong for Joey? Maybe I should hop on a plane, get a feel for each program, get a feel for how Joey would fit in."

"Honey," John says. "You really need to Let Go and Let God. Present your options before the court—any one of the places we've talked about is fine—then step back and let the judge choose. This is Joey's crisis, and the outcome is not in your hands. It never was. You need to get out of the way. You've done everything you can for Joey. Believe that. Find peace, not angst, in the Serenity Prayer. Just find peace. You need to get better not only so that Joey can get better. You need to get better for you. Let Go, Sandy. Let Go.

"You can't be with Joey on his journey, but he'll never be alone," John says. "You know the poem, 'Footprints in the Sand'? 'When you saw only one set of footprints, it was then that I carried you.' Well, who do you think has been carrying Joey all this time, through the attempted suicide and the overdoses, the car accident, and the arrests? And God is carrying Joey still. He will continue to carry Joey until he gets to the place where he can walk on his own."

The reason I called John this morning was to get guidance on what to do about Joey. What I got is guidance on what to do about me—words meant to carry me through, meant to help me survive—no matter what happens with Joey. Thanking John for his time and words of wisdom, I tell him he lifted a huge weight from my shoulders.

"You are worth it," he replies.

This man who's given me so much is a man I've never even met.

Like the story of the crusty old fisherman doggedly throwing one starfish at a time back into the ocean, undaunted by the multitudes stranded on the beach before him, John makes a difference to each life that he touches. I am one of those starfish.

⁂

Letting Go is a process. A slow and creaky process; the prying of sticky fingers off places where they don't belong. Letting Go takes real determination. And time. I dropped a letter in the mail to Judge Lee with my recommendations for substance abuse facilities, but I ignored John's advice and numbered them in order of preference, along with my rationale. There are no long-term residential programs for young adults in the state of Maryland, and I believe that the right program, not the location, should be the critical deciding factor. If this is my best chance to cram treatment down Joey's throat and make it stay down, then cram it I will. Yes, Letting Go takes time. At least it does for me.

Joey has a new cellmate, a "nice-enough guy" doing time for stabbing someone; he also has a new attitude. When I tell Joey about the rehab recommendations I sent to Judge Lee, he gets pretty cocky. Pretty cocky for someone sleeping in a cell with a guy who likes knives.

"Fuck that. If Judge Lee sends me anywhere other than back to Sunrise, I'll stay in fucking jail."

I think Joey is so used to doing things, getting things—and getting out of things—his way that he's freaked out that things might be different this time.

Rick's high school graduation is in a few days, and Joey is mad he will miss it. He curses at me and pouts. As though I'm mean for making him sweep the chimney while the rest of us go to the ball. As though the reason he will miss his brother's graduation is the fault of anything other than being an addict and being in prison. I hurry out once inmate visiting hour ends.

The incarcerated-brother cloud was hanging over Rick's graduation, but I guess Rick is accustomed to some Joey-cloud or another hanging over his life. He didn't let it ruin his special day and week, and neither did Joe and I. We stayed away from the jail and focused on Rick and the celebration of his great accomplishment. Not only did Rick graduate from high school, but he stayed focused and stable and straight throughout, while Joe and I were sucked into his older brother's vortex of chaos. And then, on the occasions when we weren't swirling about, the ghost of Joey's mistakes haunted him as Joe and I practiced learning from our own. Growing up in our household lately could not have been easy. But, in spite of everything, Rick is a fine young man. Maybe we did something right. Or maybe, he, like Joey, is just making his own path. *Go, Rick.*

Both my boys set sail down the same river, but while Rick sailed along smoothly, something rocked Joey's boat. Some perfect storm of personality, circumstances, and genetics knocked him off course. One bad choice led to another and another and choked off even others. One choice, that first choice, changed everything.

"I am an addict. I haven't made any good decisions for years, and I've messed up everything good in my life. I had a lot of time to think while sitting in my cell. Jail is horrible, and I know for sure that returning there won't help me to beat my addiction." Handcuffed and standing before Judge Lee, Joey lifts a coverall-clad shoulder to swipe at the tears on his cheek before continuing his plea. "I need help and am ready to do whatever it takes to stay in recovery."

The crowded courtroom is still except for some sniffles. Some other mother moved by the words of this child so close to lost.

One last time, I stand up before Judge Lee. One last time, because I don't think Joey's got one more bounce.

"Joey doesn't have much of anything left. Not, I'm afraid, even time. But today presents a chance for things to change. Today I can finally do something to help him. I'm asking you to sentence Joey to addiction treatment for at least a year. Force him to get the help he needs. Addiction has taken away my son. I want him back. I ask you to give Joey the chance to make that happen."

Joe follows with a broken father's version of the same desperate plea, and then Judge Lee renders his sentence.

"I've given careful consideration to this case. Joey, you clearly need help with addiction, so I'm sentencing you to three years' unsupervised probation, enabling you to receive treatment at an out-of-state facility while still being accountable to this court. You will stay there until they determine you are done. Your probation officer will make regular arrest checks; if you stay out of new trouble, all of your old trouble will be erased. You will have a clean record at the end of three years. If not, you'll be back in jail."

"Your Honor, thank you for this decision. It has probably saved my life."

Looking at Judge Lee, I mouth my own "thank you." I'm thrilled. Joey will be in the hands of Awakening Place in Palmetto Beach, Florida. The number-one choice on my list.

Joey is free. In a giddy flurry of hugs and silly grins, we celebrate. But now we need to scramble. Today's outcome was a crapshoot, so no travel arrangements have been made for Joey's trip to Florida. My daydreams had involved a brief stop at the prison to collect Joey on the drive to the airport, so I'm not at all prepared for Joey to stay in our house tonight. I'm not prepared to throw roadblocks between Joey and drugs and alcohol and money and trouble. I'm not prepared to keep Joey from blowing his last chance all to hell before he even has a chance to get to his last chance.

We start down the courthouse steps.

"A-a-a-a-h. I need to enjoy this freedom before being caged up again," says Joey, spreading his arms wide-open and letting loose a barrage of demands. He needs cigarettes, new jeans, and some time with his friends. Rancid memories of the last night Joey spent at our house a year and a half ago on his way to rehab at Havenwood make me cringe.

"Let's keep things uncomplicated. Your dad and I don't know what we're doing. We've never had a son released from jail before. So let's go home and enjoy a quiet evening together. Please don't ask for anything. Don't ask to go out, to see your friends, or even to make phone calls. Let's focus on getting you where you need to be tomorrow and not take any chances at making a mistake."

Putting distance between himself and my words—and the words he just laid on Judge Lee—Joey trots down the flight of stairs ahead of Joe and me. He looks back over his shoulder.

"Awakening Place better give me credit for my time at Sunrise Recovery. Not treat me like I'm starting all over at the beginning. I already know what to do and I've already been doing it, so they'd better give me my freedom."

"This doesn't sound much like the guy who just told Judge Lee he's hit bottom and will do whatever it takes to get better. Or like a guy who plans to do whatever it takes to get better," I say.

"Oh, I'll do whatever it takes," Joey smirks. "But I'm the guy who knows whatever that is. And I can't do it if I'm all restricted."

Somewhere between welcoming Joey home with open arms and locking up everything he shouldn't get his hands on, Joe and I find ourselves divided and conquered.

Sucked in by reasonable-sounding requests, we are sunk before we know it. I allow Joey one phone call to his twelve-step sponsor, and Joe allows a quick peek at the Awakening Place website. I cave in and pay Joey's long-overdue restitution to the lady whose car he broke into, and Joe caves in and pays a long-overdue phone bill. I buy Joey a supply of cigarettes to keep him happy at Awakening Place, and Joe buys him some new clothes to replace his other new clothes left at Sunrise. Joe and I rationalize the irrational. We argue. We disintegrate into farcical little skirmishes (but we already know who will win).

Battle-weary from the fight against my addict son, I no longer have what it takes to even pretend to draw one more line in the shifting sand. I only hope I have what it takes to make it through tonight.

Making dinner and travel arrangements and small talk, I pretend not to notice that Joey is snug in his smugness that his parents are wimps. I pretend not to notice him sneaking off to make hushed calls to who-knows-who about who-knows-what. And I pretend not to notice that we do exactly what Joey wants and not what we believe in. Joey always finds a way to use us to his advantage. Joey is still sick. We're all still sick. We have gotten nowhere in all this time.

Verse Fifteen

AWAKENING

It's the geode, not the jewel, I transport to Florida. Hopefully, once Joey is at Awakening Place, he will chip away to find the treasure he has hidden away deep inside. *This is almost over.* A long flight, long drive, long hours, and a son possessed. *I am so tired.* But Joey doesn't notice the exhaustion dragging behind me like a string of tin cans through gravel. He's too busy gushing on about drugs. *This is almost over. This is almost over.*

I see the gnarly fingers of temptation crawling all over him. Pulling him back, inch by inch, to the very place I'm whisking him away from. Joey rambles on breathlessly, gleefully, about things that make me want to cry.

"Mushrooms. I love doing mushrooms; it's like LSD. But really, I love it all. I would do anything, any drug. Cocaine, ecstasy, whatever I could get my hands on. Yeah, I would get crazy high and do crazy things." I don't want to listen to Joey, but I can't leave his side until our journey is over.

"Once I ran into the street and punched a moving car and don't even know why. I got high or drunk every night. I lied about someone dying once so I would have a reason for getting drunk when I was supposed to be getting sober. I spent everything I earned on drugs and alcohol instead of food and bills. I was stealing from people at work and dealing, but still, sometimes I didn't have enough money. So sometimes I had to use sketchy drugs. Getting high was all that mattered."

The sweet memories of high times cling to Joey like smoke from a joint. He talks on and on about the addiction of friends, the mystery of addiction, the wonder of drugs, the legalization of drugs, and the lowering of the drinking age. Everything and anything that seems to keep the mostly one-sided conversation going. *This is almost over.*

I stretch out the fingers on one hand, then the other; my grip on the steering wheel has been too tight. Barely noticing the palm trees and sunshine, I listen as Joey spins fairy tales about his upcoming months in court-ordered rehab confinement.

"I'm going to get a job right away. I need money. I think I'll find a job on a boat and become a dive master. Also, I'm going to buy a motorcycle. Maybe a Harley." Joey looks out the car window for a moment before looking back at me. "And I will get an apartment as soon as possible."

None of these things can happen, of course. Somebody once told me that addicts live in a fantasy world because they cannot deal with reality. If that means they present outlandish scenarios as though they might actually transpire, then Joey is living in a fantasy world, unable to face his reality.

Pulling the rental car into a parking space at Awakening Place, I'm relieved to see an attractive enclave of brightly colored buildings, flowering bushes, a shimmering pool, and freshly mown lawn. It looks like a nice place to leave my son. Joey sees it differently.

"I thought this place was going to be closer to the beach. I'm taking quite a step down in the world."

I now understand what John meant when he said Joey might find himself getting into recovery at the Salvation Army in ten years. *Joey will get himself sober once what he is, what he deserves, and what he needs are all in alignment.*

Friendly faces greet us, directing me to the admissions office and pointing Joey to the place for putting out cigarettes. As I write out the first month's payment of $14,000, Joey is in a small room with the door closed, doing whatever it is he needs to do to prove he's not under the influence. And then, we hug. Another goodbye.

"Mom, I'm sorry for all the trouble over the past month."

Month? How about years? I turn and leave Joey, yet again, in somebody else's hands. Pretty sure I've passed the baton for the last time.

I have a memory of Joey as a golden-haired cherub toddling around the yard, bottom-side plump and topside tippy. He bends his little self to look closely at a bug on a leaf, but topples over instead, his diapered bottom plopping on top of the first yellow daffodil of spring. Joey had no idea of the beautiful thing he crushed back then. Just as he has no idea of the beautiful things he has crushed now. Love and relationships and me.

I meet the team who will help Joey in the months ahead, including the family therapist, Danita, who will help Joe and me. *If we think, act, and react in harmony with a healthy recovery, Joey has a greater chance at success.* As we sit with her for a while in her tiny office, she somehow sweeps up the bits and scraps of what I sort of already know and puts them into words.

"Addicts want what they want and they want it now, and they will use any manipulation to get it," Danita says. "They know what buttons to push, how to deflect issues onto someone else, and how to split families. Anything is fair game. Addicts will say and do anything to get pity, get attention, deflect attention, and sidetrack emotions. They will say and do anything to melt your avowals of strength and Letting Go. Anything." *Wow.* Danita speaks as though she has already met my son.

"Joey is not a victim. He doesn't need you to fix things for him," Danita continues. "He needs to feel the brunt of what addiction has done to his life. If the impact is softened, he can't learn from it, and if he doesn't learn from it, he will repeat it." She confirms what I already know in my heart. "Joey needs to understand that a few weeks of good behavior won't lure you back into his web of manipulation. He thinks he's independent, but in reality he relies on and uses everyone around him. He needs to become independent in thought and action. You and Joe need to let Joey know he's on his own in his recovery—whatever his recovery looks like." I fidget in my chair, not sure I like where this is going.

"You need to stop sending mixed messages and taking half measures. Joey needs to know, unequivocally, that you will not rescue him ever again. He needs to know you won't cancel another trip or miss another event or abandon his brother or rearrange your lives in any way to deal with his dramas. Even if he ends up in the hospital again." *Gulp.*

"Until you and Joe work yourselves over to that kind of thinking and behaving, Joey probably will not get better," Danita says. "When you and Joe jump in to 'rescue' Joey, it's more about making yourselves feel good than it is about what's good for him. You've done all you can and said all you can. Now Let Go."

We've had Joey rehabbed and therapized, and we've immersed our own selves in support groups and family programs and books and books and books. We've twiddled around with courts, hospitals, and jails, and steered, cajoled, and negotiated until we've driven ourselves mad. For three years. But Joey is not a marionette we can control with words or wishful thinking. Our actions are not his actions. Our pulling the strings isn't the same thing as him doing the work. What we've done is give Joey a stage for going through the motions. What we need to do is to clip the strings.

"Joey needs to realize he is where he is—with what he has or doesn't have—as a result of his own choices. Do not send him any more clothes. Whatever he brought in his backpack is fine." Oh. I guess once Sunrise Recovery ships his things home, I'll just pile the new boxes on top of the old boxes in the garage. Another layer Joey probably won't ever return to claim.

"If he needs something to wear, there's a nice thrift shop down the road, a place in line with what he can afford. Once he's earning money, he can pay to have some of his things shipped here if he wants. In a few months Joey will get a job with insurance, or he'll have the income to pay for it himself." Danita leans forward. "If he gets fired or quits or loses his insurance for any reason, do not intervene. Do not start paying for his insurance again. It's not your business. Joey is an adult. You must have high expectations for him. For your sake and for his."

As I fly back to Bethesda, the balancing touch of Danita's extended hand lingers. My confidence grows, knowing her hand will continue to be there when I need to grab it. Joey is expected to remain at Awakening Place for the next nine to twelve months, during which time Judge Lee will receive regular reports. Joey will not be able to make any phone calls for now, not until his manipulative impulses are under control. And drug talk is not allowed—the retelling of "war stories" gives addicts a vicarious high and a validation they don't need. I think Awakening Place is just what Joey needs.

He is going to hate it.

Joey has been substance-free for almost three months. But while sobriety is a slippery wad of gum poked into a hole in the dike, *recovery* is a whole lifestyle and mental makeover.

The wisdom behind the Twelve Steps, the backbone of a strong recovery, shows up in hundreds of slogans. There are no shadows around these words to hide in. These words are written by the people who know, for the people who need to know, and that includes both addicts and the people who love them.

- There are only two things an addict doesn't like: the way things are and change.
- If you fail to change the person you were when you came in, that person will take you out.
- Winners do what they have to do; losers do what they want to do.
- If you're coasting, you're going downhill.
- Your bottom just may be six feet under.
- Look for a way in, not for a way out.
- Shut up, show up, and say "yes."
- Half measures avail us nothing. Not half of something. Nothing.

Walking up the hill from the mailbox, I sift through the mail. An invitation; I open it. It's not to a party or event of some honor. No, Joe and I are invited to join an event thrown by the state prison for families of released inmates. Well, I may be the mother of an addict, but I will not be the mother of an ex-con. And so I will not RSVP.

Reports come in from Awakening Place. Joey isn't internally motivated to be there, and he loathes the program. He wants to leave, isn't actively participating, and has demonstrated the capacity for spectacular tantrums, drama, threats, and manipulation. When Joey did an exercise recognizing the people he has used and manipulated over the years, Joe and I were not on his list. *Imagine that.* Joey doesn't seem to have any mental illness. The long-ago depression diagnosis never stuck. Instead, Awakening Place is focusing on Joey's deeply ingrained patterns of addicted thinking—including narcissistic and grandiose behaviors, and the poor way he treats other people—and they are pushing him to look inside himself for what brought him to where he is. But Joey is putting his efforts elsewhere.

"Recovery is an ongoing process. It takes a lot of serious work, and Joey needs to take it seriously. His success—or failure—is his choice." I listen to Danita give me the terse telephone update. "Joey needs to understand that prison or homelessness are his only other options. You and Joe need to come to terms with the idea that this is the very last time you will pay for Joey's treatment. Some addicts use treatment as a way to have a roof over their head; Joey may be one of those people."

Joey toys with his recovery at Awakening Place, but I'm both physically and emotionally removed from the drama.

I think I finally get it.

If Joey sneezes, I'm not the one who should leap for a tissue. And I'm not the one who should want to. If I'm going to help Joey, I need to Let Go—not with just one hand, not only some of the time, not only when someone is looking—but really, truly, completely Let Go. Sort of like Joey needs to Let Go of addiction. But I can't do anything about that, so I'm going to do what I can do about me.

The counselors at Awakening Place encourage letter writing during the phone call hiatus. Real letters, with real feelings, with real truths. I sit down to write my son one of those letters. I want to be honest and loving, but there's no way to be honest without also being brutal, because that's what these years have been. I write. I lessen my load. I pile Joey's mess where it belongs, on his shoulders, not mine.

All along I've been expected to face reality, deal with it, buck up, and move on. But now that I'm really ready to Let Go—to lighten my soul and unpack my baggage—I can see how it might look to others: heartless and selfish and cold. It even sort of feels that way. But there's nothing cold about it. Getting to Letting Go has been a long walk through the hottest fires of hell.

Sometimes an important moment stands on its own, but sometimes it comes rolling in, stuck to the side of a well-traveled snowball. Maybe I would have gotten to where I am anyway, but without Awakening Place I don't think I would have known my time to trust and surrender is now. That's all I ever really needed to do.

Awakening Place may or may not be where Joey finds his own awakening, but it has already stirred an awakening in me.

Verse Sixteen

THE ELEPHANT

Dear Joey,

I haven't written because I really haven't known what to say. I didn't want to write a chit-chatty letter because that would make it seem as though everything was fine, as though everything that has happened hasn't, as though you are on vacation rather than at a vital crossroads in your life. It would perpetuate our usual manner of "walking around the elephant" in the middle of our lives, and that's not healthy for us if we hope to someday have a genuine relationship again.

It's not easy to write out my thoughts concerning the past several years. It might seem more peaceful, less confrontational, to continue to sit on them, but I think it's time to let them go. It's time to share them with you, with hopes that by opening the door to honest communication it will help you, help us, to move forward.

It's a very complicated place where love and addiction meet, especially when the addict is your child. It's a unique love that parents have for their children—it's so big that we love you to let you go. From the moment we first meet, you are loved and nurtured in preparation for the life you'll choose ahead. It's a love that doesn't diminish as time passes—it just changes in presentation as our responsibilities move from teaching you how to walk to encouraging you to walk out the door on your own. We carry our love for you unconditionally and forever, although the world where you walk may be far away from our own.

There's no expectation that parenting will be easy or that things will always go smoothly. We plug along, learning the distinction between easy love (where we're rewarded with a hug or a smile) and tough love (where the perks aren't as immediate). Love guides us in doing the best we can, but when addiction meets love, lines become blurred. We want to love the child without helping the addict, but they share the same body. Reality and mirage share the same shadow.

Your dad and I couldn't see what was happening at first, Joey. More accurately, we couldn't believe what we were seeing because what we were seeing wasn't what we wanted to believe. We'd been stepping down for so long, we just couldn't tell what normal footing felt like anymore. We couldn't tell where we were coming from, where we were going, or even that we were going downhill.

We were in denial. We rationalized and we made excuses. It was years before we stopped misinterpreting the clues and recognized the unthinkable for what it was: You are an addict. I don't know how many years this went on, because I don't know when all of this started. I don't know when exactly the real you was lost. But about two years ago your behavior became so strange, so delusional, and your life was so out of control, that we finally started to do battle with the addict that wore your face.

Your addiction consumed you, but it also consumed us and our relationship with you. Unthinkable things were happening in our relationship, and it was slow torture absorbing the pain. How could this happen when we loved you so much and you once loved us?

By finally recognizing you were an addict, we could at least take twisted comfort in knowing we weren't dealing with the real you—not the soul of the child we once knew. I know that sounds horrible, but as you fell, so did our normal thinking and expectations; we tried to find some bit of good wherever we could. Sort of like how we devolved into thinking it was a "good thing" that you had the car accident or that you ended up in jail. But this world of addiction is a crazy place; it seems like everything has been turned upside down. A world where helping you *harms* you. And where hope hurts.

We made a lot of mistakes trying to help you. Sometimes we treated you like an adult when you were acting like a child, and sometimes we treated you like a child though you're an adult. We tried warm, fuzzy love and we tried tough love. We tried keeping you from hitting bottom, bringing the bottom up to you, and getting you into treatment when we thought you'd hit bottom. And we struggled to recognize the difference between helping and enabling. We tried so hard to stay on the right side of an invisible line between helping you to live and helping you to die. Through trial and error and lack of results, we learned that nothing we did worked. You stayed the same. No, actually you got worse.

Ultimately, the last safe expression of our love for you was to be supportive in getting you help for your addiction. But even that has gotten mangled in this world of your disease. It was a shock to discover that even in periods of recovery we had to continue to make sense of what makes no sense at all—we still had to sort truth from lies, still had to look into your eyes and wonder if we were talking to you or the addict, and still had to wonder who you were.

We have been forced to accept the most painful realization of all: Sometimes love means doing nothing rather than doing something, and Letting Go is not the same thing as giving up.

Our relationship has suffered a lot of hits, Joey, but even through the ugliness, I continued to believe there was some action I could take, some word I could say, that would have the magical effect of helping you. I continued to believe the time would come—after you'd lost everything—when you would reach out for help with a humble recognition of your addiction, a heartfelt desire for change, and gratitude for the opportunity to make new choices. I believed the love your dad and I had poured over you would someday come back to us.

But the night you spent here, the night between jail and treatment—just out from behind bars, verging on homelessness, and relying on us to get you the help you need—you continued with your pattern of casting illusions to get what you want.

That was the night I finally realized that even while you are sober, you will use and manipulate me and my love for you as long as I allow it. I realized that even the simplest pretense at a normal relationship gives you tools to hurt yourself on your path to recovery, and to hurt me as well. I don't want to be used anymore, Joey.

Something made this time different. Something made it clear to me that nothing will change if nothing changes.

Maybe it was my raw agony over all we'd been through in just the past few months alone—suffering of a magnitude known only to someone who loves an addict. Maybe it was seeing that you were still sick with an addict's behaviors even though you'd been sober for several months. Maybe it was your inability to see or appreciate what your dad and I have tried so hard to do for you. Probably, it was all this put together. On top of what came before.

The life of loving an addicted child is hard to explain; it's sort of like grieving your death and fighting for your life at the same time. All while hated, helpless, and alone. It's hope and belief that don't dare come out to play. It's a one-way street of trust and open arms. It's empty words, broken promises, shattered dreams, and tarnished memories. It's watching as a ship slowly capsizes in a storm, and then waiting anxiously for it to right itself. It's nudging the baby bird out of the nest only to discover it can't fly. It's a lot of heartache, Joey. A lot of heartache has piled up over the past several years.

The lies, the stealing, the manipulating, the using. The abuse of my trust by pretending to be someone you were not, even years before your addiction became obvious to me, back when I still had complete faith in you and belief in you. The degradation of my love and care for you as you made yourself into a victim with untrue stories in order to ensnare enablers. The piles of your life stacked in the garage, abandoned and growing with each personal collapse, a constant visual reminder representing a healthy adult life that never happened. The vacancy of your spot in my life, a constant reminder of a relationship that *should have been.* The nights of roaming a dark house alone, wondering if you were dead or alive. The tears shed for my son who was dying, but for whom I could do nothing but pray. So many heartaches, Joey.

Do you remember the day in court when you spewed your hatred for your dad and me simply because we were there? You told us we were nothing to you but sperm and egg donors, and you wanted nothing to do with us.

That was when I thought my sadness had reached its limit. That was when I told you there comes a point when it hurts more to hang on than it does to let go, and that this was it. I told you I would be there when your world fell apart, when you lost everything and were ready for help. But until then, I was done. Believe me, these words were never meant to cross a mama's lips.

But there was plenty of sadness to come. My guess is you have no idea the sadness I carry and little memory of your actions that caused it. So I'm going to tell you about how your life crossed mine. Even if you don't really care.

It was several months before your worried family saw you following the sperm donor court date. Before the next inevitable crisis. And then, the crisis was drunk driving, with you close to dead. Surely, we thought, this was you "hitting bottom." In retrospect, I don't think it was. It was all too abstract. You heard about the accident, you heard you were fired from your job and kicked out of your apartment and so were homeless, but you didn't live any of it. The latest catastrophe—the whole mess—could be "the accident's fault" without you really absorbing the direct consequences of your actions. You were blessed to have escaped the accident with your life, without having killed someone else and without any life-altering injuries—and you were able to move on to the comfortable new world of Sunrise Recovery.

You said some things that sounded good, but it didn't appear you took any "great awakening" or humble demeanor along as you departed the intensive care unit in Florida and headed for addiction treatment in California. Without consideration of the worry, time, effort, and financial sacrifice made on your behalf, you jumped right into working the system, manipulating everyone around you in an effort to attain the standard of living to which you feel so entitled. There appears to be a fairly big gap between what you feel entitled to and what you have earned, what you feel owed and what you deserve.

We were there for Sunrise Recovery's family program, just as we have been through all of your crises—"eating disorder," suicide attempt, addiction treatments, car accident, jail, and court and court and court. Predictably, we were subjected to your anger, coldness, and sullen attitude rather than the thankful manner of someone who appreciates having people who can be counted on and who care enough to help—even though you fairly recently declared that everyone knew how wonderful you were doing except us, that you didn't need our help, ever, and that you had plenty of people who were really like family to you.

I often feel foolish, Joey. I always feel used.

When you went to jail, you were dictating your treatment terms—Sunrise Recovery or nothing. You would stay in jail rather than go anywhere else for treatment. You spent a lot of energy avoiding the realities of why you were there behind bars. You blamed the judge. You blamed us. There was no sincere appreciation of the fact that everyone in the courtroom made a huge effort to do the right thing for you, trying to get your sick, addicted self positioned to embrace that better place called life.

In your search for loopholes in accountability, you never really got it, Joey: You were incarcerated because you violently bashed in a lady's car while high and with drugs in your pocket—less than a month after another arrest—and then broke probation to go to Florida where you drank and drove and could have killed someone. Not to mention all the other probation violations the judge didn't even know about.

When the judge sentenced you to treatment and three years' probation and released you from jail, you thanked him for probably saving your life. You told him you hadn't made any good decisions for the past three years. You said you had hit bottom and needed those experiences to see this wasn't the direction you want your life to go.

Well, we hadn't even gotten down the courthouse steps before the façade slipped away and you started in with your needs, wants, expectations, demands, and assumptions. We went from having zero importance in your life to being your full-service concierges in less than three steps.

We weren't prepared for you to come to our house that
night. We weren't prepared to handle this son of ours whom we
hardly knew and who'd rarely made an effort to see us in three
years. We weren't prepared to spend the night with an addict who
just got out of jail, was heading into treatment, and had a history
of manipulation and lies. We were just reliving a lot of rotten
memories.

We remembered all too clearly the night before you went to
Havenwood—your volatility, your getting high, your hiding of
the bongs. So, we wanted to keep that night, that one night before
you left for treatment, simple and calm. We surreptitiously went
through our routine, performed on the rare occasion of your visits—
we locked up the liquor; we hid the house keys, car keys, garage
openers, jewelry, wallets, and cell phones. We didn't want any issues.
No repeat performances. Just eat, pack, sleep, and leave the next day
without any damage. We asked you to understand our discomfort
with the situation and to respect our desire for an uncomplicated,
event-free evening.

But you couldn't do that, Joey. After all we've been through
with you over the past years, but especially the past months, you
couldn't, even now, at what one would think would be your
most humble of bottoms, respect our wishes. Respect us. You
pushed. You asked if Rick could drive you to get some cigarettes—
presenting it as a great bonding time—but made no further
overtures at bonding after we said no. What were you really after?
You negotiated calling your sponsor—how could we not agree to
that?—but a few weeks later our phone bill revealed hundreds
of dollars of long-distance and international calls made to people
other than your sponsor.

You didn't care about our wishes. You didn't care about
violating our trust. You didn't care that you were pulling us in with

pretense and then walking all over us. You didn't care that you were lying. You didn't care about spending our money. You didn't care about our feelings or the emotional pain we had endured or that your actions would add more to that already heavy burden.

You seem very comfortable with just sucking us dry and making poor excuses later. I don't think you care about us at all. Except for what you can get from us. It's a stab in my heart, Joey.

I love you more than you will ever know. But I don't trust you and I don't believe you. Too much damage has been done over too long a time. There is nothing left that I can do to help you to help yourself; I know that because I have tried it all. The time has clearly come to put into action that hard-learned lesson: *Sometimes love means doing nothing, and Letting Go is not the same thing as giving up.*

I told you once to never underestimate my love for you, and this is what I meant: I love you enough to bear the toughest love of all.

There is nothing about this kind of love that feels good, but it's the situation we've been given by the choices you have made. There is nothing I would like more than to have a normal adult relationship with you, but a lot will need to change for that to happen. I guess we'll have to start from a new beginning.

There is a place in my life that is exactly your size. I hope you think it is worth the effort of filling.

This bout in addiction treatment is the last thing we can do for you, Joey. Any choices, decisions, rewards, results, and consequences are completely and totally yours. You are at a critical crossroads and this is your last, best chance at getting better, your last, best chance at a new life. You are the only person who can put together the pieces of your life—it's all in your hands.

A real paradox in conquering addiction is that the brain that is sick is the very same one that must do the work to get well. The path from old ways to new will be a winding, frustrating web of delusion, illusion, and fantasy, but hopefully you'll make the effort to walk that path for the one person you will be spending the rest of your life with. The very worthwhile you.

In recent letters you've been fondly recalling family vacations, vacations that aren't quite so fondly remembered by me. Have you forgotten the drunken scene in Puerto Rico? And that I was forced to give you an ultimatum of "stay sober or don't stay"? As for skiing in Utah, you were moody, unpredictable, and disrespectful, and you didn't share even a moment with your uncle to express some long-overdue sympathy for the death of his wife, your aunt. You wanted nothing to do with us. Except what you could pull from our pockets.

You've expressed in letters your dislike of the way Awakening Place does things and your desire to return to Sunrise Recovery. We've also received reports that you want your lawyer to get you out of there and are trying to somehow quash the reports from Awakening Place to the judge. Whatever you do is up to you. You have complete and total control over your life, as always. But your dad and I will pay for nothing more. We will do nothing more. We can do nothing more.

You can choose to get well while at Awakening Place, or not. You can do this the right way, or you can do this your way. You can walk out, or you can stay. You can choose to hate it there, fighting the process because you feel entitled to something different or better, or not. You can find a way to get yourself back to Sunrise Recovery and the program you hated while you were there, or not. You can find a way to support yourself in Florida, or not. You can deal with courts, probation, creditors, and bills, or not.

You can end up on the streets—homeless, destitute, and alone. *Or not.*

As always, you've been given every opportunity and you have chosen what to do with them; you will be doing the same now. Your dad and I are united in our belief that we have done all that we can for you—in fact, we've probably done too much by helping you to proceed in your illness even when our intention had been not to enable you.

While it would be wonderful for you and Rick to have a real relationship, it will take a lot of effort to get to know someone you haven't paid any attention to since he was, at most, twelve years old. Really, the only Joey he knows is the addict. When you were at Sunrise Recovery, you sent Rick a message about the girls out there. And just recently you sent him a letter saying you could advise him on "sex, drugs, and rock and roll." The disrespectful and abusive attitude you display toward women, and the glorification of this messy life of yours, is no way to reestablish a long-neglected bond; it's not healthy, for either of you. I hope that someday you will strive to be a real role model, and for a relationship that is meaningful.

Your dad and I have been good parents. We haven't been perfect, but we've been the best we could possibly be. We have warmly loved you with every ounce of our being and have been fair, reasonable, responsible, and reliable. We raised you to grow into a kind, honest, responsible adult. You had every opportunity to thrive in this world, Joey—you had more enriching experiences than most people could hope for—but something went really wrong. Somewhere along the way you became uncomfortable in your own skin and reinvented yourself, immersing yourself in the shallow waters of "cool." What was wrong with the real you?

You have in you a trove of wonderful qualities: intelligence, kindness, leadership. And you're affectionate, thoughtful, hardworking, and helpful. Some of those qualities may need to be dusted off a bit, but they're all innate and inside you.

I hope that you can find something from your past to help you move into a better future.

I love you, Joey, forever and always.

I'm keeping your place warm.

Love,
Mom

Part Four

❧

Once upon a time I was just a regular mom, stumbling
through parenthood like everyone else—and then I had to
figure out how to be the mom of an addict. I had to figure
out how to love my child without helping to hurt him,
how to grieve the loss of my child who's still alive without
dying, and how to trade shame and blame for strength.

To be the mom of an addict is to be an
ambassador of truth and understanding.

No more shame. No more silence.

~SANDYSWENSON.COM

Verse Seventeen

PATCHING THE HOLE

Dear Mom and Dad,

You have the wisdom to Let Go. I love you for it and cannot imagine how hard it must be. But I've learned that Letting Go doesn't mean you're abandoning me. It means you can't live my life for me and must take care of your own. Letting Go is love. I love you so much.

Joey

Tucked into the envelope, nestled between his handwritten words like the remnant of a long-ago rose, is the essence of Joey. A thoughtfulness as natural as breath. Tucked into the envelope is the love of a son setting his parents free to let him go: "Letting Go is love."

I love you, Joey.

And so, I Let Go.

It's been two months since Joey wrote that letter. The time in between has been stormy—the same as every other time he's been in addiction treatment—but this time I'm a different kind of mom.

This time I believe in what I need to believe in. This time I'm not letting go of the Letting Go. Not even when the roiling of Joey's ocean threatens to pull me under. Like now. No, I'm tightly hanging onto the Letting Go. The Life Ring. The One Solid Thing with the great big hole. I'm tightly hanging onto the thing I can never let go of because of the thing I've already had to let go of. My addict. My son. I'm hanging onto the Letting Go because Joey must find his own hidden hero. Because in the end, the never-ending end, it comes down to what it always comes down to, but keeps getting messed up. Only Joey can do what it takes to survive. Only Joey can do it, or Joey will die.

I've heard it said, "If you can't remember your last high, you might not have had it." I don't think Joey has done either. Had it *or* remembered it. Joey is on the verge of leaving Awakening Place. He's ready to walk away from the help and the hope and the order of the court. He wants to work in a restaurant serving alcohol and doesn't want anyone telling him that what he wants might be wrong. He wants to go back to the before instead of ahead to the after.

What is wrong with the brain once so right? *Maybe caustic juices of addiction have trickled into the crevices, decaying even the most elemental functions. Like thinking.* What makes him think Judge Lee isn't going to take notice? Or, what makes him not care? Maybe the sultry slut of addiction is seducing Joey, pulling him back into relapse without him even being aware. Or maybe he is purposefully slinking his way back into scabby arms, seeking comfort there. Maybe Joey just recently heard the call of his old friend, or maybe tickly whisperings have taunted him all along. Maybe when Joey picked up his pen to write the words "Letting Go is love," he wasn't setting Joe and me free, but was, instead, flicking us off his shoulder so when relapse time came we would leave him alone.

Joey is sabotaging his recovery. Swapping halo for horns, depending on whom he is trying to trick into what. The folks at Awakening Place don't know this, but I do. I know more than any mother should. I know this because of my pipeline, my online lifeline. I know that for the past few months Joey has been sowing the seeds of relapse—lying, cheating, and sneaking around—and those seeds are now sprouting legs, ready to walk out the rehab door. This has to stop. Both Joey's destructive deception and mine. It's time to confess that I've been hovering over Joey's shoulder like a snooping old ghost.

I can't do this. I can't give this up.

I can.

I must.

Pacing the house, I call Awakening Place to confess what I know about Joey and how it is that I know it. During the conference call, the recovery team doesn't pass judgment on me, not out loud anyway, but Joey will soon get an earful. So, this is it. And this is huge. *Joey will change his passwords, putting an end to what I was unable to put an end to myself.* It's time; I no longer want a window with a view of Joey's slow death. I no longer want to see what I can't do anything about. By finally confessing, I've detached my last attachment—plucked my stubborn old barnacle off the bottom of Joey's boat—the wretched connection that's been keeping me alive while at the same time keeping me sick.

Oh, no! What have I done?

No, what's done is good.

I feel unburdened. Emboldened. Empowered. I may not be able to do anything about Joey, but I *am* able do something about myself.

Relieved of one shadowy secret, I take a look in the corners and decide it's time to clean house. I decide to sweep out my own addiction, the one that up until now I have viewed as a choice.

⁓

"My name is Sandy and I am a smoker."

I've been a smoker for most of my life. I remember with fondness my first puff on a cigarette at age thirteen, so glamorous, so grown up, and my first puff on a candy cigarette long before that. I've had plenty of good reasons to quit smoking over the years, and a couple of times I even did—when pregnant and while nursing—but I always found better reasons to quit the quitting. To Joey and Rick I explained that I was the perfect example of why they should never start smoking. *So honest and open. And weak.*

Now I want to be the perfect example of how to quit. I want to be an example of doing the right thing and sticking with it, no matter how tough. If I expect this from Joey, I need to expect the same from myself. I want to be an example of unhooking myself from the Great Big Thing with the Great Big Claws. Of untwisting myself from twisted rationalizations. Of moving ahead, one determined day at a time. Of never giving up and never giving in.

It won't be easy; there's a certain comfort in the familiar even if the familiar is uncomfortable, something I suppose every addict knows. My habit is part of who I am—a socially unacceptable closet smoker relegated to smoking outside on the porch all alone. I greet the day and the snow or sleet or rain with a cigarette in one hand and my robe clutched to my throat with the other, and I wind down my evenings the same way. Sometimes I pine for my porch—wishing for guests to hurry up and leave, or hurrying to leave non-smoke-friendly places—desperate to smoke a cigarette in peace. I've felt some shame in hiding my stinky old sin, in skulking around in dark corners and dousing myself in perfume and mouthwash, but mostly what I've felt is the need to smoke. I've had a thirty-five-year love affair with smoking—I will love it every single day for the rest of my life—but I will stop.

There's a devil in me. I know the words it will whisper; we've conversed before. *Go ahead, you've had a hard day, just smoke one.* But I can't smoke just one, not ever. Because one is never just one. One is the start of another twelve thousand mornings of "I'll quit tomorrow." And that cannot be. So, as of today, I am a nonsmoker. Forever. Today it is clear; I know what I want and won't throw it away in a moment of insanity tomorrow. I will do this; I will change, whatever it takes. I will Let Go of this thing that diminishes me. I will do the same work I want Joey to do. I will live the example. I will be the change I wish to see.

When I go to the family program at Awakening Place next week, it will not be to convince Joey to stay there. I will be there to take care of what I can, and should, even if Joey doesn't. It means there will be some recovery in this recovery. No matter what.

Life has ripped a great big chunk out of me, but I'm patching the hole.

Prior to my departure for the family program at Awakening Place, Danita prepped me over the phone. She said it takes only two minutes for a misguided parent to undo months' worth of addiction treatment progress, and to keep in mind that Joey is not away at camp—I shouldn't greet him with a squealing dash across the parking lot and a gleeful spin. She said not to lose sight of how Joey got himself there, or the devastating effect his addiction has had on his life. And mine.

Well, that part is easy. But the rest is hard.

Joe and I are the veterans in this circle. The jaded parents, the beaten parents, the parents Letting Go, while the others are still Hanging On. The others, the still hopeful—the parents who look and sound like we did not long ago—to them our Letting Go doesn't look a whole lot like love. They haven't yet been dragged through the dark places we've been dragged through. They haven't yet been pummeled into submission. No, they haven't yet been whittled down to the point of understanding that Letting Go *is* love.

The room is spacious, tiled, and cool despite the summer sun's hot rays streaming through the wall of windows. But our small group doesn't pay much attention to anything beyond our conversation.

"Parents should have zero tolerance for relapse. Tell your addicted children—and mean it—that a choice made to relapse is a choice made to go forward on their own," says Ned, the addiction counselor facilitating our group.

Following some discussion, someone coughs up the fur ball stuck in the collective-other parents' throats.

"I can't do what Joe and Sandy are prepared to do. I'm not as strong. I can't close the door on my son if he chooses to use drugs again because I want him to know he is loved."

Ouch. Letting Go *is* Love. But it also is Hurt. It is to sacrifice what feels good to oneself for what does good for another. It is to set high expectations, firm boundaries, and real consequences. It is to make an abiding, and painful, commitment to someone else's future. To Let Go is the Holy Grail of parenting done right. But when the child is an addict, what should be a very natural (learn-as-you-go) transition becomes a confusing mess.

I didn't get to Let Go of Joey the way a mother is meant to—no weaning away from the way-things-were, no creeping over to the way-things-will-be. One day I was doing regular mom stuff and the next I was doing battle with a beast. Joey and I didn't get to explore new pathways or wear new ruts in our road. We never had a chance. In so many ways, Joey's addiction has taken away so much—in so many ways, the birth of my son keeps on dying—but of all of the breaths of the thousands of little deaths, the saddest loss may be that I no longer know what it means to be my son's mom.

Our addicted children join the parents. It's group therapy time. All of them are in their twenties and thirties, but they behave like the young teens they were when they started using. Back when their maturity got stuck in adolescence. Gestures, styles, vocabulary, interests. It is disturbing to watch, but even more disturbing to realize they have no idea they are stunted.

In response to Joey's toying with the program, his therapists give him one week to choose not to relapse. To choose *not* to return to "the good life" (the hard life), the street, and jail. What I see doesn't fill me with optimism. Joey lacks not only humility and surrender, but fear. He doesn't believe his dad and I have really Let Go or that a choice to lie down in the gutter is a choice to lie there alone. If he did believe, he'd be quaking. So, I dig deep for the last words I might ever speak to my son.

"Joey, you've been sober for six months, yet I still look into the eyes of an addict. I know relapse is calling you, and so you need to understand what it means if you do." My words quiver as they shake themselves loose. Words I hope will shake something loose in my son.

"Today may be the last time I ever see you alive. I hope you make good choices. I hope you do whatever it takes to get yourself better. But if you do choose to leave Awakening Place, you'll be throwing away treatment for the last time—at least the last time your father and I will pay for. If you throw away your recovery, either I will see you again once you find your way to becoming an honest, responsible, sober person sitting at our Thanksgiving table, or I will see you at your funeral. There is nothing in between. Not anymore. I will do nothing, ever again, to help the addict because, if I do, I have no hope of ever seeing my son. I love you, Joey. And it is because I love you that I am done."

And then Joe, a broken father, says his goodbyes, too. Reflected on Joey's face is not the pain of our pain, but the writing on the wall: The addict will leave Awakening Place. It's just a matter of time. Before heading for home, Joey's addiction counselor, Ned, pulls Joe and me aside.

"You could see it in the eyes of the other parents—families live in terror of saying what you had to say to Joey, and many never will," Ned says. "But, as hard as it was, you did the right thing for him. The pain and courage don't end here, though. Joey will need to see your resolve. He'll need to see it continually reinforced over the next months and years, especially during the times he's in crisis." Ned puts a hand on Joe's shoulder. "Remember, recovery can happen even if it doesn't happen within the addict. It may not be what you imagined—or even what you thought you were working toward—but your own recovery is a successful recovery. You need to come to terms with what addiction has done to your family, and you need to grieve." He turns to me now. "Go to your parent support group, talk, pray. Do whatever it takes to find strength and peace, because what you face won't be easy. What lies ahead will come, and what lies within will find a way to come out—whether you are prepared for it or not. So, find a way to be prepared."

⌒⌒

For a long time now, I've watched as one of my most valuable jewels rolled round and round and round, getting closer and closer to falling down the drain. Well, I've just heard the clunk.

Awakening Place has told Joey to leave. For the past month, Joey's recovery team has been extending him rope to pull himself up with—but instead, he used it to hang himself. Joey sabotaged another patient's recovery and was "trafficking in contraband." The squatter residing in my son's soul has won.

"This is for the best, Mom. I want to work the program on my own," Joey tells me over the phone.

"Good luck, Joey. *Really*. You held a promising future in your hands and you have just let it go." I am unable to say any more. I am unable to stand any more. I sit on a bench outside the church I was in before my phone vibrated and I recognized the number. I knew it would be bad news, and ran out to answer it.

"Whatever happens now, he needs to own it," Ned says after Joey passes him the phone. "If no one intervenes to soften the blows, Joey might feel what a mess he's made of his life and finally, really, want help. You have no obligation, financial or otherwise, to Joey, ever again. Do not send him a plane ticket or help him to find his way back to Judge Lee. If Joey wants something badly enough, like his favorite drug, he always finds a way to get it. He can find a way to get the things that are good for him, too. He needs to want them. He needs to believe they are worth working for." I keep listening, even though I don't want to, kicking the orange and red leaves on the ground at my feet.

"Joey can work his way back into our free aftercare program if he wants to, and you need to believe that he will. This is a backward step, but it is still a step in Joey's recovery. Joey will be in the process of getting better for a long time. Not a month, or year, or even a couple of years. And it won't always be forward motion." Ned pauses. Maybe waiting for me to respond. To say something. Anything. But I cannot speak. He continues. "Do not get sucked into Joey's catastrophes over the coming years. Don't alter the direction of things or aid him in any way. Don't give him advice or even ask questions. If Joey gets into trouble, it will be through his bad decisions and choices. Don't get drawn into the emotional and psychological web. Don't settle for a fake, one-sided relationship. And take care of yourself. Knowing where Joey is and how he is doing does not help you. Nor does it do anything for him."

Joey has out-manipulated life for so long, I think he thinks he can also out-manipulate death.

Frosty fingers of fear creep through my belly, something that happens only when something is really wrong. Like when there's no handle on the escape hatch. When there's no cord on the parachute. When there's no wishful thinking left to grab onto and it's clear that things won't turn out well.

Life is totally different now. I look in the mirror and wonder why *I* don't look totally different. *Why don't I look dead?* But Joey almost always manages to look okay, too, no matter what his condition, so appearance is an indication of nothing. I am a mother waiting for her son to relapse and overdose and die. I knew it would come to this. I knew I would be pushed to the hellish hinterlands of Letting Go. But I'm not prepared. I'm not prepared to think about Joey homeless or overdosing or in prison or dead. Not yet. I'm stuck on wondering why he is so stupid.

A few months ago, as Rick packed up boxes to take to his new dorm, he asked me if Joey would ever be okay, maybe even someday go back to college himself. I told Rick I didn't know how things would turn out for Joey. There was no way to know if Joey would do the hard work or make good choices, if he would be college-bound, sober, or even alive. It was a hard truth, one Joe didn't think I should have shared. But I didn't want Rick to think everything was guaranteed to turn out fine simply because Joey was in rehab. And I didn't want Rick to make his own choices lightly.

I call Rick now to update him, catching him between classes. I tell him his brother is not okay.

"He might call you asking for money. Don't fall for his hard-luck stories, don't believe anything he says. I'm doing the same. We don't want to help him die. Just tell Joey not to call you again until he gets himself better."

"I sent Joey a letter yesterday. Maybe he'll still get it. Maybe it will help," Rick says.

When I hang up, I cry. I cry for Rick, who's missed out on having one of life's most faithful friends and a special act to follow. I cry for Joey and all the pain he's endured from those demons scratching around in his head. I cry for me. I cry for Joe, our family. I cry because the very one needed to make our family whole is the one who doesn't seem to be able to do anything but keep making everything worse.

I am prepared to allow my child to die. Because getting close to dying may be the only thing that saves him—if it doesn't kill him. Or me.

I'm chasing something, something I need, something just out of my reach. I run and run through the night and pelting rain. I run until I can go no farther, until I stand at the edge of a cliff. Bracing against a blustery wind, I lean over, looking down into black, churning water and across to the place where the thing is that I am chasing. The place too far away to see. The place I need to be. Wobbly and exhausted, I now face a journey much harder. Much scarier. I need to fly alone through the dark, tossed and whipped and battered, fighting rough waves that are sure to reach up and pull me under. I need to find the courage to keep going. I need to find the strength to make it to the other side. I am afraid. I want to give up. But I know I need to get to the thing I am chasing. Whether I want to or not. Suddenly, it's clear. I will make it, no matter what happens along the way. So I take a deep breath and I take a big leap and I fly.

Letting Go is love.

I can do both, and I can survive.

Verse Eighteen

DOWN IN MY
HEART TO STAY

It's been a long time since anybody asked about Joey. Nobody knows what to say anymore, after seven spiraling years. Time passes, and Joey quietly fades away.

I wish I hadn't taken for granted the ordinary events of everyday life—I wish I could remember the summer smells of the orchard we strolled through hand-in-hand, picking fuzzy peaches. Or if it was the elephant's big nose or the hippo's big nostrils we talked about most on the drive home from the zoo. Or why I secretly longed for a day that didn't involve another peanut butter and jelly sandwich. I wish I had more consciously savored the moments from those longest days during those shortest years. The moments I thought would be unendingly replenished.

I wish addiction never walked in our back door, and that our son didn't grow up to be an addict.

Addiction is not just a word. Not just one note. *It's a tragic symphony.*

Joey's Uncle Brian lived under a bush. I saw the packed earth and flattened weeds where he laid his head. He lived there, or under a neighboring bush, for years. An earthen lair within walking distance of the soup kitchen where he ate his meals, the homeless shelter where he broke too many rules, and the low brick rehab center he skirted. Brian now lives in a nursing home. One too many strokes from too much cocaine. Brian is fifty-six. He looks seventy-six. He moves like he's ninety and acts like he's four.

At one time, Brian, Joe's brother, was a talented chef with a rakish grin and big plans. But the man he was meant to be was destroyed by addiction. A posse of enablers helped to carry Brian into middle age. They gave in, handed out, set up, and fixed up until they became unable to enable. Or unwilling. Or burned out. By then Brian was so diminished by his addiction that he couldn't handle the business of running his life. Hence, the bush, the packed earth, the flattened weeds—the place he slept for so many years.

Following one of many medical crises, back when he could still walk unassisted, Brian walked away from a residential facility, three square meals a day, clean sheets, and a bed. Shuffling and mumbling, he went back to the streets and the drugs. Joey, at twenty-five, is where Brian was when he was in his forties.

Of the people I know who have suffered from addiction, the ones who have risen like a phoenix from the ashes faced tough love early on. I soft-loved Joey too often, fooling myself that I was helping him. The weight of my mistakes keeps me grounded.

I'm learning to live without Joey, but like someone whose leg has been amputated, I often reach for the place he once was without thinking. There's nothing phantom about the pain. There's no way to separate the void before me from what has been left behind; Joey may have been hacked from my life, but he's with me every step of the way as I try to move forward.

Before Joey became an addict, he liked me more days than he didn't. Actually, we were chums. But once addiction took over, Joey recoiled from me, and from the mirror I held up to his face, like a vampire shrinking from daylight. Now he calls only his dad, checking every once in a while to see if there's anything left to yank on. Like a used tissue, I serve no purpose and have been tossed aside. I try to ignore my hurt feelings.

Days, weeks, months, years. I wait for Joey to hit a bottom that will bounce him back into my life, a life that I have started to recover. I've joined a women's club, a book group, a drawing class. I've learned how to build a website, and I volunteer at a homeless shelter cleaning rooms. Joe and I travel. We remove Joey from our will; he must not have access to money that will help him to die if we die before he does.

Joey starts to call me once in a while. *Three steps forward. Two skinned knees back.* Always a different phone number and a different set of circumstances, but really, the same old story. He has lost more friends, more jobs; he sleeps wherever he can find a place to lay his head—and nothing is his fault. More overdoses, more detox centers. More halfway houses where he works to earn the spot that will help him stay sober, and more times he gets kicked out. More bar fights, suicide attempts, and run-ins with the law. He talks about big moves and big changes but actually just scuttles about from one nearby town to the next. If he has anyone left in his life at all, it's because he is using them or they are using him or they are just plain *using*.

"Yeah, I'm living a crummy life. I use so I don't have to see it. There's no point in getting sober if life never gets any better," Joey tells me over the phone.

"Joey, I don't want to be part of your manipulation. If you want to talk about other things, that's fine; but otherwise, we'll need to say goodbye for now. It's up to you."

Maybe Joey will lay down his first brick, something to build a recovery on, if I keep laying down mine.

Keeping the days busy, I attend lectures and go for long walks with good friends. I read and discuss good books. I don't seek out information about Joey's troubles anymore, and I keep the old stockpile tucked far back in my mind where I can't easily rummage through it. Even when new trouble calls.

"The whole rehab thing is just a moneymaking bunch of shit. I'll never go to another fucking halfway house. They're all rip-offs. They're dirty, dangerous places full of people who relapse. A fucking addict passed out on the sofa with a fucking syringe still stuck in his arm. Seeing that shit makes everyone want to relapse. It made me relapse. The Twelve Steps are a fucking racket. A cult. It's full of fucking hypocrites who won't help me, and it doesn't fucking work. And drug treatment is just brainwashing shit. You've been fucking brainwashed into not helping me; well, all that does is hurt me. I'll never have anything to do with any of it ever again. I'll find some other way to quit using. On my fucking own."

My hands may be tied, but not my heart.

Or my mouth.

"Joey, you and I both know there's nothing I can say or do that will help you or make you sober. I wish I could put my hands on your brain and shuffle things around and make you think and do the things you need to think and do in order to get yourself better, but I can't. Only you can do that. I can't do anything for you, Joey, except love you. I may be sitting on the sidelines, but I'm your biggest cheerleader; there's nobody rooting harder for you to make it back to the other side."

"I don't know why I fucking bothered to call you. It was a fucking waste of time."

Joey is so hostile, I'm afraid he'll know only darkness until the day he dies.

⁓

In the garage looking at Joey's boxes, I stand in the tailwind of Joey's long, sad, dance with addiction. The decimation of his life is piled here. I've been unable to touch the frozen jumble because I've been waiting for Joey.

But he's never coming back.

It's time to take a step forward.

There was a time, back when all this started, when I'd wanted to go through Joey's things; I'd wanted to see what I would discover, *uncover,* about Joey and his life, but I hadn't the stomach for it then. I still don't have the stomach, I no longer have the desire, and, somehow, I've acquired the wisdom not to go sticking my heart in with piranhas. So I lug Joey's boxes to the street without even looking at the potent relics inside. But

I know what's here. I know the significance of the college folders, all
neatly labeled but empty. A blue-and-yellow ski jacket with crinkled lift
tickets on the zipper. Board shorts and board. Fishing poles and fishing
magazines. Towels from his dorm and a blender from his first apartment.
Swiping at the tears rolling down my dusty face, I Let Go. Some more.

*But Joey! In my heart, I'm still holding your hand. Can you feel it? Do you
even care?*

Several times a week I go for a jog in the morning. I'm running away,
in a way. Getting stronger and faster. Rick starts jogging, too. He comes
home from college on a Saturday to run the Capital Crescent Trail with
me, eat some lunch, and do some laundry. We've run several 5K races and
are working toward a 10K. A few steps forward, together.

A homeless guy sits on the sidewalk holding a cardboard sign scrawled
with a black marker: "Hungry. Please help." He's about Joey's age. Blond,
scruffy. Fidgety. I don't believe he's hungry only for food. A man in a suit
walks by, almost falling off the curb as he tries to stay as far away from the
dusty derelict as possible. I used to assume beggars were bad. But now I
think of Joey; he has made a cardboard sign of his own at least once. I see
things differently now. Part of me wants to give that addict-boy a hug, and
the other part of me wants to shake him and yell, "Do you know what
you're doing to your mom?"

Sometimes my phone rings and I end up talking to Joey accidentally
because I don't recognize the number. Sometimes my cell phone shows it's
Joey calling, and even though I know I shouldn't take the call, I need to
hear my son's voice.

"Hi, Mom. I just got out of state detox, haven't used anything for two
days now, and am just trying to figure out where to go from here. I was
homeless and living on the beach for the last two months; I was drinking
to get to sleep and drinking shots in the mornings so I didn't have a seizure
or DTs. But one morning I was running late and couldn't get a drink, so I
had a seizure at work. That's how I got into detox. I need some money so
I don't have to go back to the bad things and places that will take me back
to a bad life."

"Joey, I'm not going to give you any money. I'm not going to give you
anything at all but my love. You have, inside you, whatever you need. A

few months ago you called with basically the same story, just a different twist of the knife, and your dad and I gave you basically the same answer: no. You found a way to get yourself into a halfway house then, and, as usual, you found your way out. I told you this before, but I guess you don't believe it: I am done trying to help." I take a deep breath.

"One more thing: The only time you call is either when you want something or want me to believe something. Never do you call just to talk. This hurts too much. From now on we can talk about the weather and family and friends and dreams—anything except yet another supposed recovery. Recovery is actually very quiet, Joey. I will know you are in recovery when I see it. I don't need you to tell me. I've heard your lies. I'm not going to have hope again. Hope hurts."

"I understand, Mom. I guess it's like loving someone who's been in remission from cancer but then has a relapse."

"No, Joey. Unlike the disease of addiction, cancer doesn't destroy the love in relationships. With addiction, I sit empty-handed watching you kill yourself. With addiction we each walk through hell alone."

I hear Joey groan.

"I'm in survival mode, Joey. I'm doing what I need to do to take care of myself now. I will not, I cannot, pick the fresh scabs off my psyche, off my barely healed wounds. So, I love you, but all I can do for you from now on is to wish you good luck."

"I thought you'd say that, Mom. Well, I hope I can figure something out."

Sometimes Joey communicates by text. I can't *not* look.

```
Mom, I have become a monster I don't even
recognize anymore. I'm sad doing this to
myself, to you all, to my friends. I don't
want to anymore. I just want to be better. It,
unfortunately, is a choice and I can't blame
not making it in on someone else. The only
reason I have to miss you all is because of me.
I can intellectualize getting and staying sober
forever, but the monster is taking over. I know
```

```
there is help. I just have to get it soon. I
know I'll be dead if I don't. The doctors told
me that on top of the amount I drink, my liver
can't handle it after the damage from the car
accident. So hug-toss. I love you so much,
always have and always will. I'm afraid I won't
last much longer if I keep doing what I'm doing.
I want to stop but don't think I can.
```

I can't stop the image from scorching my mind: *Joey lying in a morgue with a tag on his toe, his body awaiting identification by his next of kin.* I walk to my closet and push aside hangers, looking for something black that's not formal and still fits. I may need it soon. I need to be ready. I will not be capable of shopping if I get the call I am dreading.

Back when I first quit smoking, I secretly lit up and inhaled every night; it was a long time before I stopped puffing away in my dreams. I still sidle in close behind a smoker on the sidewalk for a deep whiff, but that's as close as I will ever get to a cigarette, because quitting was too hard. To start would mean having to quit again, and I don't think I could do it. Besides, I'm still trying to be a good example for Joey, even if he isn't paying any attention. Someday he might.

My access to Joey's online activities dried up long ago, with the confession of my snooping sins, but one spy-hole remains. I follow his postings on social media. He writes—and removes—his thoughts and deeds at all hours of the day and night, so I must check his page every hour, sometimes more, to glimpse the scary postings before they disappear. I go to my computer for a quick peek between curling my hair and putting on makeup. I pull out my iPhone for a peek while standing in the checkout line at the grocery store. I peek at Joey's page from bed in the middle of the night when I wake up to go to the bathroom. I don't want to do this—I am obsessed, and it makes me feel sick. I need to stop but can't. I've tried. And I can't de-friend my own son; that is a step this mom can't take.

But I can get Joey to de-friend *me*. I decide to go out with a bang. I sit at my computer and post my motherly missive right on Joey's wall, for all his friends to see. Not *to* him but *for* him:

> To Joey's friends—Because I Love My Son: Joey is an addict.
> Please do not be an enabler. Learn about addiction. Do not
> help the addict to kill my son.

Joey replies:

> Leave me alone. You're not in my life anymore and haven't
> been for a while. Stop posting on my wall. Goodbye.

Joey doesn't de-friend me. He simply removes my post. I guess it's not so easy for a son to de-friend his own mother, either. So I try again. I try again to get Joey to get rid of me. I try harder. I go bolder. Again, for all his friends to see. Again, letting the Letting Go slip. I post on Joey's page his most recent mug shot alongside a photo from somewhat better days. "This is what addiction has done to Joey in just one year. Please back off. Joey has to do the work, but you can help by letting him *need* to do it."

NOW I've been de-friended. Joey sends me a message:

> You know what fuck you. I think I cared about my pet rat that
> was homeless more than you care about me. You chose your
> life. What came from it chose *his* own life, too. You brought
> me into this shithole and I'll get myself out of it. Luck is gone.
> You know as well as I do I'm dead in a week.

I thought I had no hope left, but I just felt it slip. So I guess I still had some hope somewhere down deep.

⁓

After thirty years of marriage, Joe and I are getting divorced. Although Joey's addiction strained our marriage, this has nothing to do with that. Joe is moving in a different direction and I am shattered. A family of four, and then three, and then no longer a family at all. I don't know what happened. I gain more than a few pounds. Insomnia. Anxiety attacks. The doctor prescribes Xanax, but I don't want to become an addict.

I reach out to my mom and dad, my brothers, sisters-in-law, friends from India, my friends here in Maryland. I reunite with my college roommate and grade school girlfriends with whom I played dolls. I reconnect with friends from when I lived in Spain and my long-lost cousins. I build a foundation of strength from these people who mean something to me as they make room for me in their lives.

I breathe. I cry. I breathe. I weep. I breathe. Then, just when I think I've pulled myself together, my next breath or word or laugh turns into a sob. I'm surprised and I'm mad. *Where did that come from?*

What's not pulling me under keeps pulling me *in*. Another day, another email. Another girlfriend, ready to wash her hands of Joey, but not quite ready to wash him down the drain yet.

> I know this will be kind of a random message from someone you don't know, but I wanted to try to give you some peace of mind with Joey. He's been staying with me at my mom's house where we have been keeping him out of trouble. When I heard Joey was homeless and living on the beach I took action and gave him a place to stay until he gets back on his feet. Joey seems sad when he talks about how he hasn't had a relationship with your family lately, and has been talking about going up there for Thanksgiving. In the meantime, I'm doing my best to take care of him and help him in any way possible. I really feel like good things are on the way with Joey.

A deep voice awakens me in the night.

"Mom."

I sit up, expecting to see Rick standing by the side of my bed. But he isn't. It wasn't Rick's voice I heard; it was Joey's. And he isn't standing here, either. He's in trouble somewhere and is calling home base. I feel Joey's aloneness. He's rolling around in the gutter, an inner demon as his only friend, and is sending a signal via the umbilical tom-tom that he needs something more.

My influence cannot be constrained to the selection of Joey's casket. His disease needs to be counterbalanced by the obstinate presence of love. There's nothing I can say or do to stop Joey from doing what he's doing, but he needs to have a reason to stop. I will not give him advice or a sympathetic ear or even believe a word he says, but as long as Joey is alive I will find ways to leave traces of love along with my Letting Go. Like the sticky little handprints Joey left on my heart so long ago.

⁓

Joann is Joe's sister by blood, but she's my sister by choice. We sit at her kitchen table, cups of coffee half full, still in our jammies at noon. Every spring I come to Florida for a few weeks to soak up some sun and some sisterhood. Tomorrow we will drive to see Joey. He's only a couple of hours south of here. I haven't seen him for two years.

We laugh and laugh at everything, as always. I'm laughing still as I reach out to answer my phone.

"Mom, I'm kinda fucked."

I'm not laughing anymore. Joann asks what's wrong.

"I can't see you. Don't come down. I was nearly choked to death on a drug bust; I was an undercover informant. I've been drug-free, but I have to keep moving around. Trying to stay out of sight. Everyone knows I was the informant, and so I keep getting beat up. The guy was arrested for attempted second-degree murder, dealing LSD, Xanax, Ecstasy, and he had a shotgun." Joey sounds high. Or something . . .

"What's wrong?" Joann asks again.

"The guy who choked me is also my friend. He's like a priest, very holy. We were dealing together for about four months, until I had my spiritual awakening. I was tripping when I turned him in—the angels told me what to do, and I listened. The top of my head was like literally opened up, and an angel poured in God and goodness. LSD is a miracle, Mom. It doesn't hurt people; it helps them. They find God. It's not dangerous like meth. LSD isn't addictive, and it's only illegal because nobody understands it. It's twelve-step meetings and rehab without all the money and the miserable time. For about $25, I'm with God."

"I love you, Joey, but goodbye."

⁓

I don't write in my journal anymore. Well, not about Joey. It's no longer cathartic.

Only you will be with you every day of your life. Right now you need to make decisions just for you and your future, decisions that will leave you whole and happy. I once said this to Joey. Now I say it to me. I'm going to do whatever it takes to make my life whole and happy. Dammit. My life and heart may be broken, but I can stop the shards from damaging anything more.

Out of my need to do something, fill something, and be something, the Bistro Boyz program bloomed. I was given a seed to nurture, and a team of Bistro Galz from the Junior Women's Club of Chevy Chase (JWCCC) helped it to grow. The National Center for Children and Families (NCCF) is a nonprofit organization in Bethesda that, among many other good works, cares for young men removed from their families. Something unfortunate happened and they were plunked down in our neighborhood; that is all the JWCCC needs to know. These young men, ages thirteen to eighteen, are somebody's sons. We open our arms to them as they pass through our backyard; they will not remain invisible.

Every week a small group of Bistro Boyz and Galz grocery-shop and cook and share a meal together. We have a budget; we look for deals; we squeeze tomatoes. We chop and we talk and we wash and we stir and we bond.

Marlin grates a block of cheddar, careful to keep his knuckles out of the way.

"Miss Bonnie, is this right?" Marlin asks one of the Galz. Four middle-aged women and four teens bump elbows in the small dorm kitchen. Julio minces and measures garlic with Miss Vicky. We make a savory marinade for our budget steak and a smorgasbord of toppings for our baked potatoes. Salad. Kool-Aid.

Miss Ginny and Perry work on a cheesecake with cherries on top. This is a feast. Kevin helps me to set the long table. Knife and spoon go on the right; fork and napkin go on the left. We use paper plates tonight since the cupboards are empty. Dinner plates are either dirty or in someone's room. *Huh. Just like home.* Running two electric grills and the microwave oven all at one time blows a fuse, but we figure it out.

Once the table is laden with platters and bowls, we all sit down together.

"Before we start eating, how about if we each say something, anything, we are thankful for?" I say.

I am thankful for the fun evening of cooking. Miss Ginny is thankful for her favorite team's latest win; we discuss this glorious moment for a moment before continuing. One of the Boyz says he is thankful for learning how to cook this meal. We talk about the election and Kevin's swim meet and our next menu and the date-magnetism of knowing how to cook.

"Hey, this is sort of like being a family," says one of the Boyz.

My heart warms.

This is what I need.

To support this program, JWCCC publishes a cookbook with recipes from local restaurants and businesses and luminaries. We start a scholarship fund for Boyz interested in pursuing cooking as a career. And for the Boyz moving on to independent living, we provide boxes full of kitchen supplies like pots and dish soap and spices and an indoor grill. Something to get them started; something to remind them of a happy day in the kitchen; something to remind them they matter.

For whatever reason, the mothers of these young men aren't able to do mom stuff for them right now. But I can. And maybe someday someone will do the same thing for Joey.

⌒

A phone call in the dark of night is never good. I look at the clock on my nightstand. 5:00 a.m.; I don't answer. Silence. Then, one last jingle. A message. I pull my pillow over my head . . . one minute . . . two. . . . then fling the pillow off and listen to the slurred and mumbly recording. It sounds like Joey's mouth was barely open and full of rocks.

"Mom-m-m, I love you. Fuckin' nineypercen chance Imgonna be in jail t'night. I din do nything wrong. So. At least. Like. T'night, don' do shit for me. I'mokay. Just like pawn me off on somebody else. Loveyoumom, have a good night, good-bye, and I'll see you on the other side."

I'll see you on the other side? My heart pounds. It pounds for two hours until I call Joey back to see if he is dead. His latest girlfriend, another faceless stranger, answers. He had used her phone to call me.

"Joey was crazy last night," she says. "He's locked in my room now; I had to sleep on the floor out here. He has taken over my home and my life. He's punched fourteen holes in the walls and kicked three doors down. He had told me he was a crack addict before, but I thought he was over that. I thought he was a lightweight because when we would drink beers at night he would get really drunk, but then I found out he was drinking vodka on the sly. And one day I walked in and he was sitting on the end of the bed shooting up heroin. I kicked it out of his hand. I can't get rid of him. He hasn't paid rent for over a month, he lies all the time, he's violent. Goes nuts, throwing things and burning my paintbrushes. He's like a boy I used to babysit. I can't take care of him anymore, and I've been telling him to find someone else to mooch off of. I can barely feed myself. I don't want to get him in trouble, though. I don't want to call the police. I don't want him to be homeless. I want to help him."

"Drop him at the emergency room; there are people there who can help him. Joey knows what to do if he wants help," I say.

"I've done that before, but he always comes back."

A few days later, she texts me:

> He went crazy again so I called the cops and they
> took him away. He's mooching off people from his
> work now. I kept asking him to leave; he would
> never have left if something dramatic didn't
> happen, so I'm kinda thankful in a weird way.

With excruciating precision, addiction has plucked out every trace of the son I gave birth to. And every last tear from me.

```
Just got released from hospital. Baker-Acted.² If
you wanna do something, get a greyhound ticket
in my name so I can get outta here. Local free
help didn't do anything. I gotta get back to
where I at least know people who will help
me. Incident involved alcohol, a football, our
road, "suspected vandalism," and then a Joey who
doesn't like cops much.
```
 [Text message from Joey.]

```
Oops, that last message wasn't meant for you.
```
[Text message from Joey.]

Sometimes I don't get out of my pajamas for a whole weekend. I don't comb my hair. I tell friends I have a cold or make up some other reason for why I can't go for a walk. Really, though, sometimes I just can't cope; sometimes I just need to wallow. But I wallow less than I used to. More days than not, I'm working on making something better of my new life rather than letting the tumbled hopes of my old one take me down.

⌘

```
Happy Thanksgiving, Mom. Hopefully someday I'll
give you a reason to be thankful for me. I love
you. Thank you for still loving me.
```
[Text message from Joey.]

Something has changed in my son, the son I long ago quit swooping in to rescue or fix. While sitting on a Greyhound bus, escaping his troubles on one side of Florida and returning to the place he'd not long ago run away from on the other, Joey read a draft of this story on the tiny screen of his cell phone. Ever since then he's been calling me—knowing now, *believing*—that all I have left to give him is love. I

---

2 Florida Mental Health Act. Emergency or involuntary commitment to a mental health facility.

know Joey might be sitting there on the other end of the phone with his feet propped up on a keg and smoking a joint—no part of me believes everything will now be smooth sailing and happy and fine—but right now we have a relationship.

Joey doesn't ask for anything anymore or dump his messes in my lap. Instead, we talk about world events and he asks about my life and we keep it brief. His calls are sporadic. Sometimes when he calls he sounds slurry, so I ask him to call back on a day when he's doing better. Joey doesn't yell and swear at me like he used to; he simply agrees and hangs up. And then, in one day or one week or one month, on a day that he's sober, Joey calls back. Something has definitely changed. It's not the relationship I dreamed of with my son, but it's more than I've had for a long time and more than I thought I'd ever have again.

Joey sends me a friend request on social media. He's ready to undo the de-friending, but I don't know if I am. I don't want to be sucked back into my obsessive looking over his shoulder routine, even though part of me wants to look and see what's going on. I think about it for two weeks before I respond with a call.

"Joey, I am always your friend, but I can't be your friend on any of the social media sites. It isn't healthy for me to see what's going on in your life, so let's just continue doing what we're doing, okay?"

I move into a condo, a historic renovation of an old girls' school, with turrets and a ballroom and a pagoda. I love my new home. I hang pictures and organize closets and paint a mural of cracked stucco and exposed stone on my bathroom wall. I've had lots of practice in making a house into a home, but this time it's my home all alone. Photographs of Rick and Joey sit on the bookshelves. For a few years I had to put Joey's photos away, out of sight, out of mind, but I can look at them now. I can look at the happy old memories as gifts to be treasured, not collectors of tears. Well, usually. I'm getting better.

It is dark and quiet when my cell phone lights up with a text. Another spectral girlfriend, passing the Joey baton.

> Hi, sorry to burden you. This is Joey's
> girlfriend. I thought any parent would want to

know what's going on. I tried helping Joey so
much, to the point of destroying myself. He won't
take the help; he is currently homeless, fell back
off the wagon. I brought him to the hospital/detox
center tonight, he agreed, and then physically
attacked me again in the parking lot. I had
to leave him there; he is very violent when he
drinks. I don't know anyone else who loves him
and don't know where he will end up. I'm sorry
I couldn't do more. I have been letting him back
into my life after many violent attacks against me
and beating my car and putting 5k worth of damage
to it. I am sorry but I have to walk away for
good. I just thought someone should know. I don't
know what tonight will bring for him. I hate to
tell you this and am sorry. I love your son very
much. I wish he loved himself. I will pray for
him and your family.

I text her back:

Thanks for letting me know. I understand. It's
very hard to realize that only he has the
power to change his path. It's very hard to
let go. You've taken a strong position tonight.
Whatever happens tonight and going forward is
in Joey's hands. But I hold him in my heart.

She replies:

I feel if I didn't try to get him help it
wouldn't have gotten so bad. I feel it's my
fault. My brain knows it's not, but my heart
feels different. I know he is a good boy

under it all. Please know I tried and whatever
happens tonight I am sorry.

Me:

He's an addict. We cannot fix him. You've tried.
Be strong in knowing that.

Her:

Thank you. I am sorry you have been through so
much. If only love could cure someone.

Me:

Yes, if only. At least he knows he is loved.

Her:

I can't stay around and try to protect him from
himself while destroying myself, but I will
pray. I hope you get your son back one day;
he's lucky to have you. Thank you for talking
to me. I feel very guilty. He won't remember
this night, but we'll never forget. Good luck
with your new home and book and article. When
he's sober, Joey is so proud of you.

I tell her:

Take care of yourself. And try to shake off the
guilt. You're heading in the right direction.
One last parting word: you don't deserve to be
hit, not ever. No matter the excuse. One hit,
walk away and never ever look back.

She ends with this text:

```
Thank you very much. As we both know, the
glimpses of the boy you raised are beautiful,
but glimpses aren't enough. Goodnight, and
again, I'm sorry to burden you.
```

My goodbye:

```
This is a burden I've carried for a long time.
I'm stronger now.
```

I toss and turn. But I don't cry. I've lost and mourned Joey too many times. Something twangs somewhere near my heart, something I recognize; it's my body doing routine maintenance and spontaneously wringing out the collected sadness. I look at the clock. It's after midnight. I fall back to sleep.

```
Arrested. Baker-Acted. Now out of detox. Amazing
experience, so grateful. I love you very much
Mom. Going to half-way house. I'm starting over.
Love you. [Text from Joey.]
```

I shouldn't have hope; I don't want to have hope. I hate hope. But I have a little of it.

I'm a whole lot stronger than I was when my world first started falling apart. And I'm much more aware. I know I cannot change anyone other than myself. I know I can and will try to do the right thing, no matter how difficult. I know my capacity to love can be bruised, but not broken. And if Joey's tide starts to drag me under, I know I need to fight to escape the life-sucking pull, quickly moving out of the way until I'm safe. Remain calm. Take deep breaths.

I'm not ashamed of Joey. I'm sad for him. And I'm not ashamed to be the mother of an addict. I will no longer behave as though addiction is a dark secret, and I'm not going to live like a cockroach hiding under a rock.

I will be open and honest about what addiction has done to Joey and to our family. Like Joey, I have choices. And I choose to *live* life.

All I can do for Joey now is love him. Love him and hope he will be drawn to recovery the way a wildflower rooted in the shadows stretches toward sunlight.

But today I have today.

Things may get a lot worse before they get better—or maybe just get worse—but today is a day I will consciously savor. I still have a miracle to hold in each hand. Rick is plugging along nicely, and Joey, well, he's alive.

A song isn't a song until you sing it.

Well, *The Joey Song* has been sung. Every last note.

From the place where I live. The place where love and addiction meet.

The story doesn't end here, of course. Joey's addiction, whether he is in recovery or not, will last forever. No matter where the addict takes my son, my love for Joey will follow. No matter what happens, I will try to put joy where Joey should be.

I've got that Joy, Joy, Joy, Joy down in my heart
Down in my heart
Down in my heart
I've got that Joey, Joey, Joey, Joey down in my heart
Down in my heart to stay.

CPSIA information can be obtained
at www.ICGtesting.com
Printed in the USA
JSHW020405040822
28796JS00002B/2

9 781937 612719